Summer of the Seventeenth Doll

Insight Text Guide

Anica Boulanger-Mashberg
Ray Lawler

Copyright Page from the Original Book

First published in 2012.

Insight Publications Pty Ltd
89 Wellington Street
St Kilda VIC 3182
Australia
Tel: +61 3 9523 0044
Fax: +61 3 9523 2044
Email: books@insightpublications.com.au

www.insightpublications.com.au

National Library of Australia Cataloguing-in-Publication entry:
Boulanger-Mashberg, Anica.
Ray Lawler's Summer of the Seventeenth Doll / Anica Boulanger-Mashberg.
9781922004048 (pbk.)
Insight text guide.
Includes bibliographical references.
For secondary school age.
Lawler, Ray, 1921– . Summer of the seventeenth doll.
Lawler, Ray, 1921– . —Criticism and interpretation.
A822.3

TABLE OF CONTENTS

CHARACTER MAP

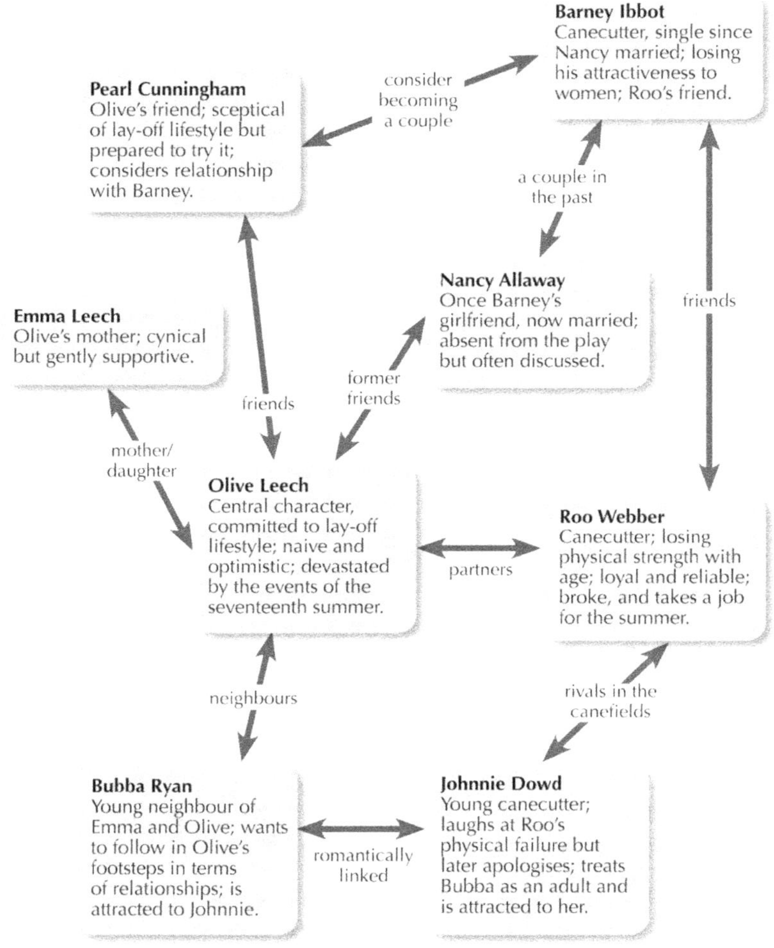

Barney Ibbot
Canecutter, single since Nancy married; losing his attractiveness to women; Roo's friend.
consider becoming a couple
Pearl Cunningham
Olive's friend; sceptical of lay-off lifestyle but prepared to try it; considers relationship with Barney.
a couple in the past
friends
Nancy Allaway
Once Barney's girlfriend, now married; absent from the play but often discussed.
Emma Leech
Olive's mother; cynical but gently supportive.
friends
former friends
mother/ daughter
Olive Leech
Central character, committed to lay-off lifestyle; naive and optimistic; devastated by the events of the seventeenth summer.
partners
Roo Webber
Canecutter; losing physical strength with age; loyal and reliable; broke, and takes a job for the summer.
neighbours
rivals in the canefields
Bubba Ryan
Young neighbour of Emma and Olive; wants to follow in Olive's footsteps in terms of relationships; is attracted to Johnnie.
romantically linked
Johnnie Dowd
Young canecutter; laughs at Roo's physical failure but later apologises; treats Bubba as an adult and is attracted to her.

OVERVIEW

About the author

Ray Lawler is an Australian playwright who has contributed to the development of Australian theatre not just with his written work, but also as an actor and director, and through his ongoing association with the Melbourne Theatre Company. Born in Melbourne in 1921, Lawler has been based in Australia for much of his life, although he has also lived overseas for extended periods. His plays often explore Australian characters, settings and concerns.

He is married to actress Jacqueline Kelleher, whom he met when she was playing Bubba in an early production of *Summer of the Seventeenth Doll.* They married while on tour in 1956, and they have three children.

Summer of the Seventeenth Doll (1957, first performed in 1955 with Lawler himself as Barney) is Lawler's tenth and most successful play. In the late 1970s he wrote two other plays about the same group of characters – *Kid Stakes* (1978) and *Other Times* (1978) – which, with a revised version of *Summer of the Seventeenth Doll,* form *The Doll Trilogy* (1978, first performed in 1977). *Kid Stakes* is the first in the trilogy, introducing the characters, and set in 1937 during the summer of the first doll.

Other Times is set in 1945 during World War II, and *Summer of the Seventeenth Doll* concludes the trilogy.

Synopsis

Summer of the Seventeenth Doll (often known familiarly and affectionately as *The Doll)* is set in Melbourne during the summer of 1953–54. The action of the play takes place in Carlton in an old two-storey house which is the home of the elderly Emma and her daughter Olive. The play spans approximately a month, beginning in early December and concluding a week into the new year.

At the opening of the play, Olive's young next-door neighbour and friend, Bubba Ryan, is visiting Olive's house – something she has done regularly all her life. She is chatting with Olive's friend Pearl about the impending arrival of Roo and Barney, two canecutters who have spent the last sixteen 'lay-off' seasons (December to April, when there is no cutting work) in Olive's house. Pearl, a widow who works as a barmaid in the same hotel as Olive, has been invited by Olive to join her in her home for the lay-off season this year, with the suggestion that she and Barney might make a good romantic match.

In the months preceding the play's timeframe, Nancy (paired with Barney in previous lay-off seasons) has married bookseller Harry Allaway, and has removed herself from the friendship group and from the carefree lifestyle that she enjoyed with Olive, Roo and Barney for sixteen years. In many ways, Pearl steps into Nancy's shoes, but their personalities differ significantly.

The men arrive, and Olive is thrilled to see them, but it is clear already that this year will be different. Nancy's departure has changed the patterns of the past sixteen summers, and we soon discover that there have been changes for the men too. Most notably, Roo has had a 'bloody awful season' (p.23) and has arrived broke. This doesn't bode well for the summer and when, at the end of the first scene, he presents Olive with the traditional gift of a 'doll' (a kewpie doll dressed carnival-style and mounted on a black cane walking stick), her joyful appreciation belies the destruction of tradition that is to come.

As the play progresses, we follow the development of the relationships between the characters, particularly those between Olive and Roo, Roo and Barney, and Barney and Pearl. In each case, the ultimate result is the disintegration or destruction of a friendship or relationship. We see the characters attempting to re-enact and recapture the joyous times of past lay-offs – they play cards; they repeat (offstage and between scenes) various excursions and sojourns from past summers; they attempt a jovial sing-along on New Year's Eve; they try to plan an outing to reunite Roo with Johnnie Dowd, with whom he fought during the cutting season. Roo even proposes to Olive in an attempt to hold on to their love and past happiness. But the characters are irritable with each other, the excursions are thwarted by poor weather and unfulfilled expectations, New Year's Eve ends in tears, the truce between Roo and Johnnie is terse and temporary, and Olive ardently rejects Roo's proposal.

Character summaries

Pearl Cunningham

A widow; probably in her late thirties (though her age is not specified in the text); mother of Vera (eighteen years old, lives with relations); works as a barmaid in a hotel with Olive; has been invited to stay with Olive for the lay-off season. She and Barney are introduced to each other as a possible match. Pearl is cynical and often suspicious of Olive's life, which she perceives as less than respectable.

Kathie 'Bubba' Ryan

Supporting character; twenty-two years old, but Olive and the men still tend to think of her as the child she was when they first met her. She has lived next door to Olive and Emma all her life, and looks up to Olive and to her life with the men.

Olive Leech

Olive is thirty-nine years old but has a youthful optimism that tends towards naivety. She is the daughter of Emma, with whom she lives. She works with Pearl as a hotel barmaid. Olive loves Roo and lives for the lay-off season each year, when she can spend five months with Roo and Barney.

Arthur 'Barney' Ibbot

'Barney' is forty years old, a canecutter and Roo's best mate. He has a 'weakness for women' (p.17) and has grown accustomed to winning them over easily and regularly with confidence and charm. Although he is described as a small man, this is mostly in comparison to Roo. He fought in World War II and was paired with Nancy before she married. He has two adult sons and a younger daughter – all by different mothers – for whom he has willingly paid 'maintenance'.

Emma Leech

Supporting character; Olive's mother; in her late sixties; shrewd (particularly when it comes to money and judgement of character); protective of her daughter but in a way that often comes across as sharp and brusque instead of affectionate. While she is fiercely proud of her piano playing and happily participates in the 'community singin', she nevertheless goes through life 'expecting the worst' of the world (p.17).

Reuben 'Roo' Webber

Roo is forty-one years old, a canecutter who is well respected as a ganger (foreperson of a labouring gang) and good at his job, but who is now slowing with age. He is Barney's best mate – a 'man's man' (p.18); physically large though usually gentle; proud and defensive of his own masculinity; paired with Olive.

Johnnie Dowd

A supporting character, Johnnie is twenty-five years old; he is a strong, fast canecutter taken on by Roo as part of his gang. He takes over as ganger when Roo leaves. When Dowd comes to find Roo and Barney in Carlton he treats Bubba as an adult, thus winning her affection.

Nancy Allaway

Although Nancy, a supporting character, is absent from the play's action (having recently married Harry Allaway, a bookseller), she is an important player in the history of the main characters. Nancy is often referred to, and represents the carefree tone of the sixteen previous lay-offs. She worked at the hotel with her friend Olive and was romantically paired with Barney.

BACKGROUND & CONTEXT

The Doll Trilogy

It is interesting that *Summer of the Seventeenth Doll* is the final work in the trilogy, yet the first and second works were written retrospectively – like many contemporary cinematic 'prequels' – and more than twenty years later. The first two plays in the trilogy have never enjoyed the success of *The Doll,* and while they offer us a new perspective on the lives and experiences of Emma, Olive, Nancy, Barney, Roo, Bubba and Pearl, the characters and the narrative of *The Doll* still stand alone. Moreover, the place that the play holds in the Australian cultural and theatrical psyche has not been particularly enhanced or defined by the two additional plays.

While the characters' retrospectively constructed backgrounds can illuminate the events in *Summer of the Seventeenth Doll,* they should not be allowed to colour an interpretation of the play. Director John Sumner relates some engaging anecdotes about the first production of *Other Times.* He notes, for example, that the actors (who were rehearsing a new production of *The Doll* in the daytime while performing *Other Times* in an evening season) had a tendency to 'inject the near tragic overtones from ... the former ... into their performances of the latter at night' (Lawler 1978, p.xiii). While this is a fascinating story about the challenges of such a task for the actors, it also suggests the way that information from one source can inform or, if interpreted in a problematic way, contaminate another. If you have already seen or read, or decide to see or read, the rest of the trilogy, you should be careful not to let knowledge about characters and events from *Kid Stakes* or *Other Times* seep into your understanding and analysis of *Summer of the Seventeenth Doll.*

(For more discussion of the events of *Kid Stakes* and *Other Times,* either read *The Doll Trilogy* in its entirety, or see Katharine Brisbane's essay in the Currency edition of *Summer of the Seventeenth Doll.)*

Australian theatre in the 1950s

Summer of the Seventeenth Doll is often acknowledged as the first real Australian play: it was one of the earliest Australian narratives to find commercial success in Australia and, soon after, in London too. Until then, most of the plays performed on the Australian commercial stage were either fully imported productions, or Australian productions of non-Australian scripts. Australians were not yet accustomed to seeing their own stories and their own ways of speaking represented on the stage. There was a distinct reluctance to accept the value in Australian work, or even of Australian performers. As Alrene Sykes has noted, even actor training was seen as something the young Commonwealth country was not yet equipped for, and a recommendation to the government at the time suggested that funding for 'training Australian actors in England' and touring British companies to 'raise the standards of appreciation and expectation in Australian audiences' would be money well spent (Love 1984, p.204).

When *The Doll* was produced in 1955 by the brand new Australian Elizabethan Theatre Trust, it was one of the first opportunities for Australian audiences to see their own narratives mirrored back at them from the commercial stage. It is difficult to imagine how it might have felt, for audiences accustomed primarily to American and British drama, to suddenly hear the Australian accent (particularly because Lawler wrote so boldly in the vernacular of the time and place) telling Australian stories. It should be noted, though, that the Australia presented by *The Doll* was an Australia of the working class who were not exactly the demographic of the theatre-going public, since audiences were more likely to be comfortably middle-class. As Sykes observes, it was several more decades before the Australian theatre was also prepared to tell middle-class stories (Love 1984, pp.208–9).

Publication and production history

Lawler entered his script in the 1954 Australian Playwrights Advisory Board Competition and won equal first place, which gave him a footing for the early theatrical production of his play. Australian playwrights had to work hard for any success or recognition, and awards were one way of gaining notice and credibility. Although Lawler has said he thought, at the time, that the play was a small work suitable for repertory performance, it turned out to be an important work of Australian theatre and has had a much longer life than perhaps even he anticipated. Playwright and critic Leonard Radic even says that 'the history of the modern Australian theatre begins with it' (Radic 2006, p.25).

The play continues to be regularly performed around Australia since its first production in 1955 by Melbourne's Union Theatre Repertory Company. It has become part of the canon (the most important works) of Australian theatre, capturing a vivid slice of a particular kind of

1950s Australian lifestyle. It was also adapted for film in 1960 and, interestingly, as an opera.

The choice of opera – a form usually reserved for grand, large-scale theatrical narratives with sweeping themes and spectacular presentation – might seem an unusual way to re-imagine such a naturalistic play. The opera by Richard Mills (music) and Peter Goldsworthy (libretto) is a chamber opera, using a reduced orchestration which allows the production to be more reserved than a full-scale opera. It was first performed in 1996 and was broadcast a year later by the ABC in their Sunday evening 'simulcast' (television and radio broadcast) series, notably, on Australia Day. The decision by the national broadcaster to air the production on Australia Day demonstrates the position that the play occupies in Australian culture. It captures, portrays, celebrates (though sometimes also criticises) and documents an important part of Australian history, and while not all the content is relevant today, the play remains important as both social document and dramatic text.

Historical and social contexts

The 1950s in Australia was a time of relative conservatism. Although the social conventions portrayed in *Summer of the Seventeenth Doll* may appear dated now, they reflect the norms and accepted standards of the time in which the play was written. Marriage, for example, was unquestionably the expected and accepted way of life, especially for a woman. *The Doll* presents Olive as a slightly unconventional and headstrong woman who has weighed up her options and made the choice to carry on her life and her relationship with Roo in a committed part-time fashion, spending the lay-offs with him and then continuing to work as a barmaid and awaiting his return while he works in the cane fields during the other seven months of the year. There is nothing shocking in this today, and nothing remarkable in Olive's commitment to her lifestyle. But in the 1950s, her lifestyle choices were unusual and were probably seen by many audience members not just as unconventional but even as unacceptable. Audiences of early productions were likely to be aligned closely with Pearl when it came to moral viewpoints, and Pearl clearly disapproves of Olive's lifestyle (even though she is reluctantly prepared to give it a chance herself).

As John Sumner, the director of the first production of *The Doll,* notes in his introduction to *The Doll Trilogy,* Pearl's criticisms were wellreceived by audiences in the 1950s, but by the 1970s, when *Kid Stakes* and *Other Times* were first performed, Pearl 'was looked upon by part of her audience as a wowser' (Lawler

1978, p.xiii). While studying the play, it is worth remembering the differing social values that may have been common when the work was written. However, although the play is a product of its times, it is not merely an historical artefact; when we read it today, we are analysing and responding to the characters and situations with our own contemporary perspectives. The fact that it is still a frequently produced script – by both amateur and professional organisations – suggests that the play's themes and ideas are engaging both for their evocation of an Australia of the 1950s, and for their continued relevance to contemporary audiences.

Summer of the Seventeenth Doll explores not only the moral standards of 1950s Australia, but also the social and economic landscapes of that period. For example, the characters attempt a sing-song with Emma playing the piano, a common activity then. Television in Australia did not begin broadcasting until 1956, so entertainment and socialising in the home involved different activities from those common in later decades. Families – including extended families and friendship groups like the one in the Leech household during the lay-off – had fewer means to escape each other's company, and more established habits of gathering together socially. This is something worth considering when we examine the rising tensions evident as events unfold and the characters' expectations are challenged. Although the women and Roo have jobs to go to, in the evenings they tend to be home together, which compounds any strains in their relationships and contributes to some of the conflicts they experience.

GENRE, STRUCTURE & LANGUAGE

Genre

Summer of the Seventeenth Doll is a modern realist drama. Realism in theatre has its roots in the nineteenth century and particularly in European drama, where the issues tackled were often weighty cultural and political ideas relevant to the society of the day. Although Lawler's play concerns itself primarily with the domestic, personal and psychological realities of its central characters, these are set against a broader social and cultural backdrop. Women lacked the freedom within relationships that is possible today and were constrained in their ability to choose their own lifestyle. For many men, too, especially those whose main skills and abilities lay in physical labour, personal freedoms were curtailed by the state of the economy and the societal norms and mores which dictated expectations for relationships and lifestyles.

Realist theatre is a broad genre, and although it implies a certain range of content and style, it is not bound by a concrete set of rules. Realism, most simply, is concerned with representing the reality of the artist's contemporary life experience. Realist writing for the stage, then, tends to reflect the playwright's 'now' (rather than the past or possible futures) and the cultural, geographical and social environment within which they live. Realism does not rely on grand theatricality or fantastical modes through which to present its themes. For example, the settings in *Summer of the Seventeenth Doll* are domestic, contained and as 'real' as possible – the detailed set descriptions suggest that Olive and Emma's house should look like an actual house rather than any abstract or symbolic representation of a house. Similarly, the style of acting implied by the characterisations and stage directions is 'realistic'. Moreover, the characters' emotions, while heightened, are strongly grounded in their experiences and circumstances, so that the modes of expression that the actors employ are also realistic. (See further discussion under 'Language', pp.14–15.)

Symbolism

While *The Doll* employs techniques of realism, it does also rely heavily on symbolism to convey its themes. Sometimes this is a linguistic strategy – for example, the title itself offers us a number of symbolic clues to the tone of the play. The word 'summer' symbolises a carefree, joyful freedom (much like the characters have always appreciated during the lay-off seasons, which are their most valued times). The number seventeen is symbolic of a boundary between the ages of childhood and adulthood, with eighteen traditionally representing the commencement of adulthood. These themes of freedom and youth are central to the play.

Symbolism in *The Doll* is also found in the use of lighting (see below, in 'Structure', for more discussion on this) and props. A central example of the symbolic use of props is the dolls themselves, which symbolise the idealistic, playful, youthful traditions of the lay-off seasons. They dominate the stage at the optimistic opening of the play; the destruction of the vase containing the seventeenth doll concludes Act Two with a powerful symbolic illustration of the destruction of Olive's happiness; and their absence in Act Three provides a symbolic representation of what has been lost by the characters (especially Olive) at this point.

Q Explain your understanding of realism as a theatrical style. Identify qualities of *The Doll* which support the argument that it is written in a realist style – think about themes, stagecraft, characters and style.

Q How does Lawler use other props as symbolic objects to help illustrate themes of the play?

Structure

The play follows a simple three-act structure, with a suitable place for an interval between the first and second acts. Each act is broken down into scenes, allowing for changes in chronological setting. Within the scenes time progresses naturalistically – in accordance with the expectations of the realist genre – but the blackouts between scenes allow for varying periods of time to pass, from hours to days to weeks. Although the lengths of the hiatuses (breaks in time) are specified in the stage directions, an audience has no way of knowing exactly how much time passes between the end of one scene and the beginning of the next. It is possible, however, to draw general conclusions about the passage of time from the characters' dialogue.

The traditional shape of a three-act work allows for each act to serve a particular function or functions in the overall structure.

- The first act serves an **expository function** (giving background information about characters and actions) and introduces an **initiating action** or **inciting incident** (something that unsettles the characters and generates the ongoing action of the play).

- The second act develops the characters and conflict; the **rising action** precedes the climax.
- The third act features the **climax** and **denouement** (or falling action).

For the most part, *Summer of the Seventeenth Doll* follows this pattern comfortably: in Act One, we meet the central characters and learn a little of their background. The moment we discover that Roo is broke might be regarded as the inciting incident in this scene – it jolts the characters (especially Olive) out of their otherwise-contented beginning to the lay-off, and will trigger much of the action and conflict to come. In Act Two, the relationships between characters are deepened, as we see Pearl coming to terms with the lay-off way of life, Bubba meeting Johnnie, Olive and Roo struggling to navigate their relationship under the strain of Roo's financial difficulties, and Roo and Barney dealing with the conflict that has developed in their friendship. Here the script departs slightly from a classical three-act structure: instead of taking place in the third act, the main climax occurs in the argument at the end of Act Two, Scene Two, which concludes with Roo smashing the vase containing the seventeenth doll. This means that the play's denouement is presented in the single scene of the final act.

Scene lighting as a map

An interesting way to trace the action through the three acts in this play is to examine the stage directions for the lighting design/operation. These instructions regarding the colour, intensity and mood of lighting provide interesting markers to the emotional tone with which Lawler intends to imbue each scene. The lighting directions are as follows:

- Act One, Scene One: there is a 'dominant note of cheerfully faded pink' in the room and the overall effect is of 'a glowing interior luminosity protected from the drabness outside by a light-filtered, shifting curtain of greenery' (p.4).
- Act One, Scene Two: 'Lights come up on an empty stage' (p.28).
- Act Two, Scene One: 'The lighting on the verandah and outside the house is a darkness of exhausted heat. Inside the room it is an electric, sweat-reflecting pink' (p.44).
- Act Two, Scene Two: 'the verandah is flooded with a fading sunlight that slowly, through this scene, takes on a deep blood tinge – a Russell Drysdale red – as the sun gradually sets ... the light is still strong enough to strike into the room' (p.58).

(Drysdale, an Australian painter celebrated for his work at the time *The Doll* was written, often painted Australian landscapes in overwhelming tones of deep, earthy reds.)

- Act Three, Scene One: there are no specific instructions regarding lighting.

Q Choose one of the lighting descriptions above. Explain how it helps to convey or symbolise the emotional tone of the scene, and how this fits into the dramatic structure of the play. (Think about exposition, inciting incidents, conflict, the development of action, climax and resolution.)

Language

As is appropriate to the realist mode of drama, speech patterns in *The Doll* are informal, representing natural conversation, rather than formalised, stylised or poetic, as in the dialogue of other forms of drama, such as Greek tragedy, absurdist theatre, or other heightened theatrical styles including musicals. This allows the characters to sound like 'real people' rather than the theatrical constructions that they are. For a contemporary audience, some of these speech patterns may sound self-conscious, since they re-create the sounds of an earlier era, so it is up to the director and actors to support and convey the naturalistic style Lawler intended.

In order to achieve a naturalistic tone, dialogue in *The Doll* contains elements such as:

- pauses
- interruptions
- nicknames (Roo, Bubba, Nance, Pearlie, Olly, lovey, etc.)
- slang and colloquialisms (e.g. 'oscar', 'happy as Larry', p.10; 'by crikey', p.65; words like 'shouldna', 'oughta', 'gotta', 'gunna', 'fella', ''coz', 'youse', 'p'bably') – some of which are explained in the Glossary to the 1978 edition (p.96)
- casual phrasing and articulation/pronunciation (e.g. contractions such as 'how'd you like it' and 'ain't', and characters regularly dropping the 'g' from words ending in 'ing')
- familiar reference to local and contemporary locations and events without explaining them (including Luna Park, down South, Makarandi, Selby, the Morrises')
- phonetic spellings of social/regional speech habits (e.g. 'How d'yer do' ... 'How's yerself', p.17; 'Gawd'; 'tomorrer').

The effect of incorporating these techniques into the dialogue is that the audience feels as though they are eavesdropping on the characters' conversations and lives, rather than viewing a stylised interpretation of such conversations (as might be the intention with other more theatrically heightened works). This might seem unremarkable today, but theatres up until that time had been very reluctant to present work containing the patterns of everyday Australian speech.

Q Why does Lawler allow his characters to use slang and grammatically incorrect speech patterns? What does their speech tell us about his characters? How does this aid our understanding of the themes and ideas contained in the play?

SCENE-BY-SCENE ANALYSIS

Act One, Scene One (pp.5–27)

Summary: *Olive, Pearl and Bubba await Roo and Barney's arrival, discussing past lay-offs and anticipating the summer; the men arrive with Emma and meet Pearl for the first time; Barney tells Olive about Roo's bad season, and that Roo is broke; Roo gives Olive the seventeenth doll.*

In this first scene we meet all the characters except Johnnie as we are given an overview of the previous summers – with hints about what might change in this particular summer.

We enter the action in mid-conversation, as the first line of dialogue begins with an ellipsis – punctuation representing omission or absence, or the continuation of a previous thought. The ellipsis in Bubba's line alerts us to the fact that she is mid-story. In a literal sense, we have missed part of the information (Bubba has already told Pearl who Nancy is, for example); symbolically, we realise that we are stepping into a story which has been taking place for some time – in fact, for sixteen previous summers.

In this way, the audience is aligned with Pearl, who has entered not just Bubba's conversation, but Olive's life mid-story. Pearl has stepped into Olive's established pattern of spending lay-off seasons with Roo and Barney, and working all winter without them. Like Pearl, we are about to gain an insight into the life Olive has enjoyed for the last sixteen years, and like Pearl, we do not know what will happen this year. Unlike Pearl, though, we will have access to the other characters' feelings and opinions, giving us additional knowledge and understanding that Pearl does not have. This creates dramatic irony, enabling us to foresee the changes that this seventeenth summer will bring.

Although we step into the action mid-conversation, lending a sense of immediacy to the scene, there is still plenty of scope for expository information. The audience is aligned with Pearl here, as she is a newcomer to the friendship group and to the habits and traditions of the lay-off. This allows other characters, especially Bubba, to explain things to Pearl in great detail, simultaneously explaining them for the audience, also newcomers to the story.

Although the audience is aligned with Pearl in a practical sense, she is not an immediately sympathetic character – the first stage direction describes her as *'listening rather suspiciously'* (p.5), and her dialogue in the opening pages is often sharp, defensive, guarded and even judgemental. For example, Pearl assumes that Bubba's apparently innocent comment about her not needing to read any books until after April is somehow 'nasty-minded' (p.6). She also criticises Bubba's familiarity with Olive's life, passes judgement on Nancy's character after merely seeing a photograph of her, and complains about Barney's lack of height before meeting him. In contrast, Bubba (as a representative of the other characters) appears innocent, friendly and approachable. She speaks fondly about other characters, helps Olive prepare the house for the men's arrival, and welcomes Pearl to the house and the friendship group with no sense of suspicion, resentment or anything other than gentle nostalgia about Nancy's departure from the group. Before the men arrive, then, we have learned the history of their summer visits and some of the background to the relationships and habits of the group.

Olive's explanations of the first doll and the lolly walking-sticks for Bubba (p.10) set up the importance of tradition in the play. Over the years the friends have established and maintained many little customs and routines which, though they may seem playful and superficial, all form part of their relationships and way of life. To Olive these traditions are special and meaningful, representing and even legitimising everything about the life that she loves. She wants Pearl to understand and respect them – and, by extension, to understand and respect her way of life. Pearl's 'unimpressed' silence at the end of Olive's story (p.10) indicates her resistance to the whole idea, foreshadowing her inability to settle into the lifestyle Olive leads.

Key point

In the middle of this scene, Olive provides an important definition of the lay-off season and the established pattern with the men: it is 'five months of heaven every year' and 'a time for livin'' (p.13). She explains that the men work hard for seven months canecutting, then come south to enjoy their time off. She recognises that she has sacrificed a steady and secure traditional married life to have this instead, and she has no regrets about her decision – she loves waiting for Roo to arrive and she feels that the pleasures of the five-month lay-off season more than compensate for the time she has to spend without him.

When the men finally arrive, their behaviour appears to support Olive's characterisations of them. They are playful and teasing – Barney carrying the elderly and amused Emma over his shoulder and both men calling out to Bubba to come and visit – all in good cheer that seems to signal the five months of carefree fun that Olive has described. Although their meeting with Pearl is uncomfortable, both she and the men attempt to make a good impression on each other, optimistic that they can still have an enjoyable summer without Nancy. Any discomfort is quickly dismissed; similarly, a potential conflict, when Emma complains about Olive using her vinegar, instead becomes a laughing matter as the friends tease Emma in a familiar way, demonstrating their long, affectionate history together (p.20).

Immediately following this light-hearted reunion, however, a note of sadness is introduced when Olive gives Barney a letter from Nancy. We see that Barney is still fond of her and wishes she hadn't married and left. However, Olive quickly reminds him that it is Pearl he should think of now, while at the same time warning him that Pearl is wary so he shouldn't simply assume that he'll succeed as usual. This leads to Barney telling Olive the story of Roo's bad season.

In this exchange, we see the depth of Barney and Roo's friendship. We also see Roo's stubborn determination to maintain the reputation by which he defines himself – as a man who is successful because he is strong. Here, the younger cutter Johnnie is indirectly introduced as the up-and-coming success who has already proven a threat to Roo. We also gain some insight into Roo's despair, when Barney recounts how Roo left the gang and worked his way through his savings by drinking heavily.

Roo re-enters the room at this point, displeased to overhear Barney telling Olive the story. He announces that he intends to find work during the lay-off and that he is considering staying elsewhere – both unprecedented events in the history of the group. Although Roo is stubborn, angry and bitter, he also demonstrates his genuine affection for Olive, giving the audience a glimpse of their mutual commitment which has allowed them to maintain their relationship through the previous sixteen winters. They *'hold each other in a long kiss'* (p.26), ending the scene with a return to the cheerful and celebratory reunion that Bubba's early descriptions have led us to expect. When Roo presents Olive with the seventeenth doll, she *'gives a cry of sheer happiness'* (p.27), entirely unaware of the tragedies to come.

Key vocabulary

Ganger: the leader of a labour gang – Roo works as a ganger with the canecutters.

Q Although the audience is aligned with Pearl in a practical sense – like Pearl, we are entering new territory and trying to understand the relationships and history of the past summers – our sympathies are directed towards other characters such as Bubba and Olive. How does Lawler encourage us to relate more to these characters than to Pearl?

Q The theme of custom and routine is introduced in this first scene, especially through Olive's explanation about the dolls. Can you identify three other themes of the play which are introduced in this scene?

Act One, Scene Two (pp.28–43)

Summary: *Olive and Roo clean up after the previous night's celebrations; Roo decides to get a job at the Lyman Paint Company; Barney and Roo argue about Roo trying to find work; Emma and Barney both offer Roo a loan; Pearl and Barney discuss Barney's children; Pearl cautiously commits to staying on.*

In contrast to the high energy of the first scene – particularly the laughter, raised voices, music and festive mood of the final moments of the scene – this second scene is very subdued, with little physical action. The focus instead is on the dialogue and the interactions between characters, showing us in more depth the existing relationships such as Olive and Roo's, and giving us an insight into the development of the newer relationships, particularly Pearl and Barney's.

In the opening of the scene, which takes place on the morning following the previous scene, Roo, Olive and Emma are cleaning up from the previous night's dinner. The many bottles and the wrapping paper suggest that the night was a warm and joyous celebration of Roo and Barney's return, which signifies the beginning of the lay-off season. As she cleans up, Olive reinforces this notion with her assertion that the seventeenth doll is 'prettier than ever' (p.29), indicating that she thinks the dolls have been better every year, with this year's doll particularly beautiful. Here we see that for Olive, the dolls represent the happiness of the lay-off seasons. Ironically, she anticipates that this will be the best summer of all.

In sharp contrast, Roo claims that the dolls are 'just the same as they always was' (p.29). Unfortunately, as we are beginning to realise, there are strong signs that the opposite is likely – this summer is likely to be far *worse* for him than any other. Olive, however, refuses to let Roo's words dampen her spirits, and enthusiastically describes what the dolls really mean to her. While she loves all the souvenirs he's brought down from the north, the dolls are the most significant for her because Roo has initiated the whole idea; he is not just bringing them because she's asked him for a memento or gift. This exchange demonstrates Olive's insistence that nothing has altered and that the lay-off this year will be as special as the others, highlighting her reluctance to accept that change is already evident in Roo's financial circumstances. Consequently, she continues to discuss plans as though everything is the same, asking him to book tickets to shows then to visit her at the pub where she works.

Instead it is Emma, once Olive leaves the room, who acknowledges the reality of the situation by offering Roo a loan which he turns down because he knows it isn't enough to get him through the lay-off. In typical style, however, he couches his refusal in terms of politeness and gentlemanly dignity, along with some gentle teasing: 'start taking oscar from women and don't know where you'll end' (p.33). The discussion about money illustrates the strength of the relationship between Emma and Roo, revealing her unexpected good opinion of him. That she wouldn't make the same offer to Barney implies that she respects Roo more, since he has demonstrated himself worthy of her trust with 'Olly all these years' (p.34). Emma notes that she formed her opinion of him the first time they met, deciding he was 'a packet of trouble, but ... honest' (p.34) – a fond estimation which seems to be borne out not only by his careful rejection of her support, but also by his behaviour throughout the play.

When Barney then makes a similar offer of financial support, partly out of his genuine loyalty to his friend and partly because he doesn't particularly relish the idea of spending the lay-off relaxing alone while Roo is at work, Roo's refusal is harsher and more insistent, indicating his need to maintain his independence and reputation: 'I don't want your money, I can still earn my own' (p.35).

As the play progresses, we see that it's not just money threatening the usual easy 'heaven' of the lay-off, but the changed dynamics of the group. Although Barney is still characteristically nonchalant and confident, we learn that he unsuccessfully attempted to charm and court Pearl during the night, and that his presumptions about the situation as well as his careless drunkenness did not go down well with her at all; she doesn't even wish to speak to him until Olive convinces her to try to mollify herself and give him a second chance.

Pearl and Barney enter into a long discussion about Barney's children, his responsibilities to them, the decisions he has made and his justifications for those decisions. This allows them some concentrated time to gain some insight into each other's situations (pp.36–41). With no other characters present, they speak frankly and firmly, each arguing for their perspective. Barney attempts to convince Pearl that he has behaved as decently as possible under the circumstances, while Pearl explains – from her position as a mother – why she is judging him. Although Pearl does not appear convinced at the end of this exchange, at the conclusion of the scene she casually announces that Barney might as well take her bags upstairs because she's planning to stay, at least for the time being.

The other significant exchange in this scene is between Roo and Bubba (pp.32–3). Bubba raises the sensitive issue of Nancy's departure from the group, giving Roo some photographs of the wedding because she wants Barney to have them, even though she knows Olive would disapprove. She is honest and heartfelt when she describes her regret that Barney and Nancy couldn't work things out. Roo responds with equal honesty, revealing how Barney went off on his own on the day of the wedding, so emotionally vulnerable that he was not even able to turn to Roo for support.

After this delicate conversation, Bubba nervously asks Roo whether this summer will be 'just the same' as all the past summers – the same Christmas plans, the same celebrations and pleasures. Although she doesn't yet know about Roo's financial trouble, Bubba senses that the change brought about by Nancy's departure might mean that things won't be quite the same this year. Roo, however, teasing her in a familiarly avuncular (like an uncle) style, reassures her: 'course it'll be the same' (p.33). While attempting to convince Bubba, he is also trying to convince himself; but we, as an audience, can see straight through his empty reassurances.

Key point

In this scene we see that Bubba – the youngest character, and the one the others still think of as a child – is the only character mature enough to foresee that significant changes will take place in this seventeenth summer.

Q Why do you think Pearl decides to stay at the end of this scene? What evidence is there in the script to support your answer?

Q Why does Olive react so angrily when Barney tells her Roo is going to get himself a job (p.36)?

Act Two, Scene One (pp.44–57)

Summary: *It is New Year's Eve; Olive and Roo play cards while Barney writes to his daughter's mother and Pearl knits. They all argue about whether or not to go out; Emma plays piano for a sing-song, but they don't take it seriously enough so she aborts the activity; Barney tells Roo that Johnnie is in town; Pearl criticises the lay-off lifestyle again; Olive breaks down in tears as the new year begins.*

Several weeks have passed since the previous scene. Despite the lack of detail about what has taken place in between, we are aware that the relationships have changed and that the events leading up to this scene have contributed to the tensions evident here. For example, when the scene opens Pearl is haranguing Barney about the content of his letter while he is responding angrily and impatiently. This suggests that they have probably had similar conversations in recent weeks, and similar differences of opinion. They are now less tolerant of each other and more short-tempered. The last few weeks have certainly not been the idyllic lay-off Olive has come to expect or that Pearl was led to hope for. Pearl complains, for example, about the river boat trips Olive promised and the place in Selby where they stayed for Christmas (p.49). The boat trips were ruined by poor weather, while the Christmas accommodation simply failed to live up to Pearl's standards, so there has been no real culpability on Olive's part. Still, Pearl feels that the summer is not panning out as she'd expected, while Olive feels that Pearl is too judgemental of the rituals and experiences that are integral to the lay-off lifestyle.

The hot evening compounds the tension and irritability in the house. When Bubba arrives to show Olive her dress before going off to a party, she mentions that the others *could* have gone to the Morrises' for the evening, unwittingly contributing to the friction in the room. Pearl's enquiry regarding the identity of the Morrises is the last straw for Olive, who snaps that the Morrises are cousins of Nancy's. This reply gives voice to the unspoken feeling that the negativity in the room all stems from Nancy's absence, and that Pearl's presence is responsible for at least some of the dulling of the usual lay-off festivities.

Key point

Pearl relates the story of a man in the pub describing the behaviour of migratory birds, and of Olive associating the description with the men coming south for the lay-off. Pearl's response to this is scornful – she thinks the analogy absurd. Olive is hurt by her censure, and the men are also *'not amused'* (p.48). This incident clearly demonstrates the rift growing between Pearl and the others.

The rising tensions are briefly curtailed by Barney's attempt to lighten up the evening with a sing-song, but too quickly this degenerates into argument and accusation: Emma criticises the group's effort and ability, and refuses to play any longer. Although the singing has failed to relieve the conflicts in the group, it does energise everyone, and they make another attempt to resurrect the celebrations that are usual on New Year's Eve, with Olive and Pearl heading to the kitchen to make some food. This leaves Barney and Roo to discuss their circumstances, including the fact that Barney, too, is running out of money and is considering following in Roo's footsteps and getting a job.

When Barney reveals that Johnnie Dowd is in town with some of the other cutters, he indicates that he is keen to help Roo repair his relationship with them so they can be back on track for the next cutting season. However, Barney's proposal to go to the Murray to pick grapes for the rest of the summer enrages Roo, who is furious with Barney for even considering it. Roo accuses Barney of lacking loyalty to the traditional lay-off season, revealing a similarity between Roo and Olive – their commitment to continuing the lifestyle they have enjoyed for the past sixteen years, even when times become trying. We also see how much Roo cares for Olive, when he praises *her* loyalty during the winters and comments that she was the only reason he returned south this year.

When Olive and Pearl return with food and beer, they all attempt to jolly themselves into celebrating the last few moments of the year. Once again, Pearl's judgemental view of the whole situation (this time she seems genuinely unaware that she is being critical) upsets everyone, especially Olive. The scene ends with Olive in tears and Roo beside her as the chimes strike midnight in the distance.

This scene juxtaposes the New Year's Eve setting – traditionally a time of new beginnings, great joy, celebration and good cheer – with the regretful moods of each of the central characters. Not one of them has much to celebrate: Olive mourns the loss of lay-offs past;

Barney misses Nancy; Pearl remains unfulfilled by the summer; Roo faces a reunion with Johnnie as well as the reality of his financial downfall and declining physical strength. The final moments of the scene are filled with heightened emotions – the joy of those celebrating beyond the house contrasting poignantly with the misery of those inside – foreshadowing the emotional climax of the next scene.

Key vocabulary

Ructions: a colloquial term for a disturbance or argument.

Q What significance is there in Emma's choice of song for the group to sing (p.51)? Can you relate the content to any of the themes and issues in the play?

Q In this scene Pearl gives several examples of events that Olive presented as exciting but which Pearl finds disappointing. Do you think the expectations Olive set up for Pearl were unrealistic or was Pearl unable to embrace a new lifestyle? Justify your views.

Act Two, Scene Two (pp.58–75)

Summary: *Olive and Pearl arrive home from the pub with Barney (who is drunk) and Johnnie Dowd; Johnnie and Roo shake hands; Barney and Johnnie plan a day at the races; Barney* *introduces Bubba to Johnnie; Johnnie and Bubba speak to each other alone; Roo and Barney argue; Roo makes Barney admit to Olive that the story about Roo's back was a lie; Roo smashes the vase containing the seventeenth doll.*

When Barney brings Johnnie home to Roo, it seems inevitable that the scene will escalate into conflict, given the rocky history between the two men. Ultimately the scene *does* climax with an argument, but it is between the good friends Barney and Roo, not Roo and Johnnie. Although the earlier conflict between Roo and Johnnie sets the scene for this argument, their quarrel is not the most important incident.

While Johnnie is willing to apologise to the older canecutter, and they settle into an uneasy sense of peace, the truce is more challenging for Roo, who feels that his authority as a worker and his own sense of manhood are compromised by being forced to 'knuckle under' (p.70) to Johnnie. Not only must he do this, but he must do it in the house that is usually his sanctuary; Barney has brought Johnnie 'right into this house in the lay-off' (p.70). He also has to suffer this humiliation in front of Olive – for whom he wishes to maintain the appearance of the strong, confident and successful man she has always admired. Finally, he faces further humiliation because he is in his paint factory work clothes. In Roo's eyes, these clothes provide the physical evidence that he can no longer be the superior ganger of his past, but instead is lowered to the status of a mere factory worker.

Key point

For Roo, the paint-stained uniform is a symbol of the compromise he has made. No longer able to support himself as a successful ganger who is free to spend the lay-off in relative luxury and pleasure, he must instead settle into a daily grind – that he has never envied or wanted – with a job in town. For Olive, too (although she refrains from criticising him), this job represents everything about an 'ordinary' life that she has never desired.

After the previous two scenes, this climactic scene of the play offers a heightened energy and physical activity. From the moment Johnnie offers his hand to Roo, whose *'intention could just as easily be to kill as to comply'* (p.60), the tension builds so that we expect some sort of explosion before there can be any resolution.

Barney's desperation for such a resolution is almost tangible – he clings to any idea he can come up with to reconcile the two men, changing his mind whenever he thinks he has found a winning plan. First he suggests a boys' day out at the races, but realising that alcohol and the company of the other men might not be conducive to Roo's acquiescence, he then invites Pearl and Olive, and tries to find a date for Johnnie. He initially thinks of Vera, but Pearl is apprehensive, so Barney casts around and comes up with the perfect solution: Bubba.

In fact, Barney's suggestion is better than even he realises. When Bubba and Johnnie have a moment alone, they connect easily, bonding over their shared frustration at being treated like kids by the older men and women. Bubba, especially, is grateful for Johnnie's use of her real name – a symbol that he recognises her for the young woman she is, not merely as the child whom Olive, Roo and Barney have (affectionately) talked down to for so many years. Inadvertently, then, Barney does create some good out of the situation, though it is not exactly the outcome he might have envisioned.

Roo is furious when he catches on to Barney's plans; despite Olive's pleas, he is clearly spoiling for a row with his old friend. At the climax of their fight Roo forces Barney to reveal the truth that Roo 'never had a bad back' (p.74). Barney feels that his lie is protecting Roo's reputation, but Roo insists that Olive and Emma hear the facts. The scene reaches a dramatic conclusion when Roo raises the touchy subject of Barney having failed to 'hold' Nancy (p.74). In fury, Barney tries to hit Roo with the vase holding the seventeenth doll, which Roo then grabs and smashes – symbolically destroying everything the lay-offs have stood for over the last sixteen years.

Q Why is Pearl upset by Barney's suggestion to invite Vera to the races?

Q What does this scene suggest about the effects of pride?

Q Can you think of any other ways Barney could have facilitated a reconciliation between Roo and Johnnie, considering their history?

Act Three, Scene One (pp.76–95)

Summary: *Pearl and Olive argue as Pearl awaits a taxi to leave; Roo and Olive bicker; Emma and Roo discuss the lay-offs; Bubba threatens to find Johnnie after Barney tells her the date at the races is off; Roo confesses to Barney that he isn't going back for the cutting season; Roo proposes to Olive, who turns him down; Roo and Barney leave the house.*

In this final scene we follow the denouement as the characters come to terms with the aftermath of the emotional climax in the previous scene. Conflict, irritation, regret and loss permeate the scene; there is a definite sense that more than just interior decorations have been smashed. The spirit of the lay-off has been broken, and the characters each react in their own way.

- Pearl has reached the end of her patience and leaves – she no longer holds any hope that Olive's lifestyle and friends can offer her anything.
- Bubba has seen the others come to the sad end of an era, and in response strengthens her own resolve to live the life she wants, to 'have it safe and know that it's going to last' (p.86). The life she wants is not very different from the one she has just watched Olive and the boys lose, but she desires something more enduring.
- Barney at first seems less remorseful than the others, but eventually indicates that he thinks the only way forward is for him and Roo to go their separate ways. He, too, sees that something they have had for at least sixteen years is now damaged beyond repair.
- Roo has been in stubborn denial that they are all ageing and therefore no longer able to lead the same life. Yet he, more than any other character, has come to a realisation that they have to let go of the past.

His proposal to Olive is his way of trying to move forward and make the future the best it can be.

- Olive is utterly bereft at having lost the lifestyle she loves, the value system she has built up around the lay-offs, and the happiness she's enjoyed. She is still mourning the physical and emotional destruction of the night before, and she refuses Roo's proposal in a miserable denial that she could ever settle into a 'normal' life.
- Emma is unsurprised that the happy-go-lucky lay-off years are over: the ending affirms her grim, insistent belief that there's not much to celebrate in the world.

The prevalence of conflict in this scene supports the idea embedded in the play that happiness is transient and that carefree joys will always come to an end. There are arguments and criticisms here between friends, lovers and family members, and there is little resolution.

Although Bubba's determined optimism provides a small measure of hope, the play concludes with a sense that all that was once good in the world is now in the past for this group of people. The final stage directions tell us that as Barney and Roo make eye contact before leaving the house (for what we assume will be the final time), there is '*a completely open acknowledgement of what they have lost'* (p.95).

Key point

Bubba's youthful certainty that she can live the life she wants – without it disintegrating the way Olive's has – is a stark contrast to Olive's sorrow in this scene. This reflects an underlying idea in the play: that with age comes a loss of idealism.

The play has come full circle – at the opening, we were awaiting the arrival of the men and the characters were filled with optimism. Now, the visitors have departed and, far from having fulfilled the optimism, the events of the past weeks have emptied the characters of hope and left them all (with the possible exception of Bubba and Johnnie) broken and miserable.

Q Based on their behaviour in this scene, what would you imagine each character doing in the eighteenth summer?

CHARACTERS & RELATIONSHIPS

Pearl Cunningham

> ### Key quotes
>
> 'I don't have to fit in. What I'm here for is a ... a visit, and if Olive's told you it's anythin' else...' (p.6)
>
> 'So long as a woman keeps her self-respect, any man will marry her.' (p.9)
>
> She graduates from a *'suspicious tentative approach'* to *'an assurance that is a little offensive in its complacency.'* (p.44)
>
> 'I was only tellin' you how the whole thing looked to me. If a person can't pass an opinion...' (p.49)
>
> 'Maybe I haven't been any second Nancy, but then I never set out to be.' (p.78)

Pearl is the newcomer in the group, filling the gap left when Nancy decided to marry and remove herself from the lay-off summers. The expectation is that Pearl will be able to fit into the group as Nancy did – as Barney hopes, it will be 'just like old times' (p.19) – and perhaps even form a couple with Barney (as Nancy ultimately did not). But Pearl and Nancy are very different, and from the beginning, Pearl doesn't seem to be a good match for either Barney or the group. Although Pearl and Olive share a workplace and, to some extent, a way of life, whereas Olive is content, Pearl wishes for something different.

Key point

Pearl is an outsider to the world of the lay-off season, just as we, the audience, are outsiders.

Personality

The first stage direction tells us exactly who Pearl is: *'a widow driven back to earning a living'* as a barmaid even though *'she would infinitely prefer something more classy'* (p.5). Her first line is said *'questioningly'* (p.5) and even from these two small details, we can see that Pearl is someone who is unsatisfied with her own life, yet cautious and rather judgemental about new possibilities when they are offered to her. We continue to learn about her in this first scene: she is sharp with Bubba; jumps to swift conclusions about Nancy and the lay-off lifestyle; judges others' behaviour, tastes and decisions; and is fiercely protective of her own independence, asserting her right to decide whether or not to stay with Olive for the summer.

Although Pearl has accepted Olive's invitation to join them for the summer, she is hesitant from the beginning, not even unpacking her bags until after meeting the men and still reserving her right to change her mind. She has come with expectations (based on what Olive has told her about the men and the lay-off), but nothing can fulfil them. Pearl criticises everything and refuses to see the reasons Olive has enjoyed her summers in the past.

The right thing

Pearl's daughter, Vera, is eighteen and lives 'with relations' (p.21); Pearl frequently cites Vera as her reason for wanting to do things the right way, to set a good example. She says she herself 'didn't have a chance from the beginning' and she wants to offer Vera a better life (p.64).

Because Olive's lifestyle doesn't fit with Pearl's relatively conservative concept of how a woman should live, she judges Olive's decisions and opinions even before meeting the men and glimpsing the lay-off lifestyle. She frequently forms her opinions in advance and holds on to them even in the face of evidence that they might be unfounded. When she discusses Barney's children with him, she at first assumes that he is a 'no-hoper ... must be!' (p.38), and even after their heated discussion she still feels that his 'mistakes' (the children he has fathered) are inexcusable (p.39). However, she does seem to reluctantly take on Barney's arguments, and at the end of their discussion she reconsiders her decision, casually admitting that she'll give the summer a try. In her characteristically defensive way, however, she hedges her bets, advising Barney, 'don't jump to any conclusions, there's nothin' settled yet' (p.42).

Pearl and Nancy

In some ways Pearl and Nancy are similar, and several characters note this, perhaps trying to convince themselves that Pearl will be a good match for Barney and will fit into the group as Nancy did. Olive, for example, says to Pearl that 'You're a bit alike, you two' (p.8), referring to Pearl and Nancy's physical appearance, with the implication that this somehow reflects on Pearl's ability to fit in. Barney, at the end of the play, observes that Pearl is 'walkin' out for the very same reason' that Nancy did (p.78): that she 'couldn't get what she wanted here' (p.79).

But ultimately Pearl can never be Nancy, and Olive blames her for that and for all its implications:

> PEARL: *[her eyes widening]* You're blamin' me, aren't you? Because I was here instead of Nancy.
>
> OLIVE: Yes. (p.77)

What Olive is blaming Pearl for is not only the disappointment of the seventeenth summer, but also the destruction of her illusions and the loss of all her future happiness, since the summers can never be the same again.

Q Do you think Pearl is responsible, to any degree, for the way the seventeenth summer turns out? Why, or why not?

Q Think about Pearl's name. What qualities does Pearl share with her namesake and what might Lawler hope to convey about her character through her name? Does this occur with other characters in the play?

Q From what the characters say about Nancy, how do you think Pearl and Nancy might be alike? How do you think they might differ?

Olive Leech

Key quotes

'Compared to all the marriages I know, what I got is ... is five months of heaven every year.' (p.13)

'PEARL: I figured out what's the matter with you. You're blind to everything outside this house and the lay-off season.

OLIVE: I'm blind to what I want to be.' (p.77)

'Middle of the night Olive sat here on the floor, huggin' this and howling. A grown-up woman, howling over a silly old kewpie doll. That's Olive for yer!' (Emma to Roo, p.84)

'You think I'll let it all end up in marriage – every day – a paint factory – you think I'll marry you? ... I want what I had before ... You give it back to me...' (pp.92–3)

Olive is one of the central characters, and it is she who is responsible for sharing with us (often through Pearl) the lore and lure of the lay-off. It is common for central characters in a narrative to undertake a journey in which they grow and develop; however,

Olive's journey is one of steadfast refusal to accept change, and it is this that leads to her downfall. From beginning to end, she remains idealistic about her lifestyle, committed to the existence she loves and insistent that traditions be upheld and continued. When Roo's changed circumstances make this impossible, Olive has no ability to adapt, and is thus devastated by the events of the play. In contrast, some other characters are able to acknowledge change and make corresponding changes in their own lives in order to adapt and move on.

Contradictions

Like any complex character, Olive's personality is made up of seemingly contradictory characteristics which combine to present a coherent and believable individual. Examples of Olive's internal conflicts and tensions include:

- Open-mindedness/conservatism: Olive is open to less conventional ways of life (such as her relationship with Roo, or Bubba's role in the lay-offs, which Pearl finds inappropriate), yet she is completely unwilling to accept change or compromise her own ideals. This makes her quite conservative within her own established patterns of behaviour.
- Naivety/cynicism: Olive's affection for childish traditions such as the dolls, and her belief that the lay-off lifestyle will last, re-

flect her naive optimism about the world. At the same time, she sees through Barney's bravado about his life, warning him that he'll have to work hard with Pearl, and acknowledging the pragmatism that may be required to initiate Pearl into the group.

- Fragility/dominance: Olive falls to pieces when things don't go as she hopes they will (such as at the end of Act Two, Scene One, and again at the end of the play), yet she is also a strong character who is stubborn and insistent. There is a strong sense that she has been the main force behind the traditions and happiness of past summers.

Key point

At her first entrance, the stage directions describe Olive as possessing *'something curiously unfinished ... an eagerness that properly belongs to extreme youth'* (p.7). This image of a youthful middle-aged woman exemplifies the contradictions Olive embodies.

From the opening scene, Olive is an endearing character. Her carefree cheerfulness and youthful excitement about the approaching lay-off suggest the fun they have all had in the past, and convey the warm, welcoming energy that must have led Pearl to accept the invitation in the first place. As the play progresses, though, we see that Olive is unable to modulate her behaviour, so that as the traditions crumble around her and her optimism goes unrewarded, she has no way to incorporate the new circumstances into her experience, and we see that she will be left behind.

Q Do you think Olive is a victim of her circumstances, or does she contribute to her own misery? Find specific evidence in the text to support your answer.

Arthur 'Barney' Ibbot

Key quotes

'Honest, you've never met a bloke like Barney. Only about so big, and yet – I dunno – the women go mad on him.' (p.9)

'You're always wantin' to be goin' out somewhere.' (Pearl to Barney, p.45)

On the day of Nancy's wedding to Harry, 'Barney ... went away on his own a whole afternoon, something I've never seen him do before ... he didn't even want me near him.' (Roo to Bubba, p.32)

Even before we see him, Barney is painted as a larrikin and a ladies' man. When we meet him, his jovial and teasing attitude supports this, but we also come to understand his more sensitive side. We realise that he had genuine feelings for Nancy, and that he has compassionately supported each of his illegitimate children out of a sense of duty and a desire to do the right thing. Barney is often enthusiastic though not very organised in his thinking, which can cause confusion and exacerbate tensions. For example, when he tries to reunite Roo and Johnnie he is energetic and well-meaning but does not have a clear plan, changing his mind frequently and never really succeeding in orchestrating the situation he wishes to create.

Friendship

Barney's relationship with Roo is conflicted; he has always looked up to Roo and tried to support and protect him, but he fails to see that this isn't always what Roo wants. He lies to Olive about Roo's back in an effort to maintain Roo's reputation and dignity, but doesn't realise that Roo would ultimately rather tell the truth about his situation.

Courtship

Barney's confidence leads him to court Pearl with some complacency – he assumes he will succeed with her as he always has with others. When (after some genuine attempts to foster a relationship with her) he doesn't, he is not distraught but recognises that perhaps Nancy was his one true love after all, and that he and Pearl would never have satisfied each other. Roo also refers to Barney's other recent unsuccessful attempts to woo women (p.74), suggesting that Barney has not yet accepted that his attractiveness to women now belongs in the past.

Q Why do you think Emma would not be willing to offer Barney a loan (even though she is happy to do it for Roo)?

Reuben 'Roo' Webber

Key quotes

'Roo's one of the best men they've got – runs his own gang – but even down here you never get him yappin' about his season's tally.' (Olive to Pearl, p.14)

'... *a man's man with a streak of gentleness...*' (p.18)

> 'Olive, I'm broke. D'yer understand? Flat, stoney, stinkin' broke!' (p.26)
>
> '... a packet of trouble, but he's honest...' (p.34)
>
> 'Look, I know this is seventeen years too late ... but – I want to marry you, Ol.' (p.92)

Roo is a man at the declining edge of his prime. Olive and Barney both idolise and adore him in their own ways (Olive romantically, Barney platonically), and they describe him in a glowing light. For Barney, Roo has always been a role model; he describes Roo as having been a 'sort of little tin god' to him, and states: 'I've never seen him in the wrong before' (p.24). (Note that 'tin god' refers to a person who is the object of admiration, but doesn't necessarily deserve to be. Barney knows Roo is imperfect, but still looks up to him.) For Olive, Roo is the ideal partner – she loves the time she spends with him every year, waits faithfully for him in between, and proudly tells Pearl that 'he's got the best-looking mouth in the world' (p.11). But the Roo we meet is not quite the hero Barney and Olive have known for so long. Instead, he is downtrodden; physically and financially defeated; and forced to consider changing his hopes, goals and way of life in order to survive.

Pride and flexibility

Roo is a proud man who is reluctant to admit his physical failings in the cane fields during the previous winter. He is concerned about losing face in front of Johnnie, and stubbornly insists on supporting himself, to the extent that he refuses offers of loans from both Barney and Emma. Despite this pride, he possesses the capacity to adapt. Unlike Olive, he is prepared to make changes, including:

- working in the paint factory
- cutting back on the carefree, colourful lay-off lifestyle
- giving up his itinerant life as a cutter
- proposing marriage to Olive after seventeen years.

But even Roo's willingness to adapt to his altered circumstances cannot secure his happiness: Olive rejects his marriage proposal and he is left facing an uncertain future without her.

Q Why do you think Roo proposes to Olive after seventeen years? What else could he have tried in order to save their relationship?

Kathie 'Bubba' Ryan

Key quotes

'She's been runnin' in and out ever since she was old enough to walk. Roo and Barney she treats as if they were uncles.' (Olive to Pearl, p.8)

'It's going to be just the same, isn't it? I mean, it's still going to be Selby at Christmas time, and ... and all the rest. You won't alter anything?' (p.33)

'Seems to me they're keeping you in the cradle...' (Johnnie to Bubba, p.68)

'I'll have what you had – the real part of it – but I'll have it differently. Some way I can have it safe and know that it's going to last.' (p.86)

At twenty-two years of age, Bubba is on the verge of adulthood but the adult characters in the play largely refuse to recognise her as anything but a little girl. Olive tells Pearl that Bubba is 'only a baby' (p.7), while Roo reveals his reluctance to truly recognise that she has grown up:

> ROO: *[teasing]* Strikes me you're gunna grow up to be your Uncle Barney all over again.

BUBBA: *[quietly]* I'm twenty-two now. How much more do you reckon I have to grow!

ROO: Ah, c'mon, I was only kiddin'. We all know you've left school. (p.33)

This exchange demonstrates the affection the adults have for Bubba, and also the way in which that fondness prevents them from recognising her as the woman she has become. It takes Johnnie Dowd, a fresh pair of eyes, to see her for who she really is. He notes that her nickname is the others' way of keeping her 'in the cradle' (p.68) and he is the only character in the play to call her by her real name, Kathie.

Key point

Meeting Johnnie is a turning point for Bubba, a moment when she realises that perhaps she is not completely trapped in her childish identity.

With Johnnie, Bubba sees the possibility of expressing and developing her identity as an adult, and she is keen to develop her relationship with him. Nevertheless, although she seems to want to embrace the world as an independent adult, she also hopes to emulate the lifestyle that she has watched Olive, Nancy,

Roo and Barney lead for so many years, because 'nothin' else is any good' (p.86). Bubba represents the next generation, the possibility of change and the hope that not all relationships must end in disappointment and loss, as Nancy and Barney's did, and Roo and Olive's appears to. Bubba seems determined to live her life in the same way, but the play gives us little reason to believe that she will be able to hold on to her joy any more than Olive could.

Q Does Bubba have any chance of avoiding the sad fate of the play's older characters? Why or why not?

Emma Leech

Key quotes

'Oh, she's an old shrewdy, that one.' (Olive to Pearl, about Emma, p.11)

'The lay-offs in this house are finished – for all of you.' (p.94)

To begin with, Emma seems miserly, unduly pessimistic and overly disparaging about Olive's life and the lay-off seasons. However, as the play progresses and we see the happiness of the younger characters gradually dissipate, Emma's approach to life seems to have a particular validity. Her resigned cantankerousness serves as comic relief in what otherwise is an emotionally draining piece of theatre. Yet Emma is also canny; her habit of eavesdropping serves her well and she seems to know more about her daughter and the other characters than they know about themselves.

Q Can you identify a point in the script at which we realise (before it dawns on the other characters) that Emma's cynicism about the layoffs has been well-founded? Justify your answer.

Johnnie Dowd

Key quotes

'Cracked up to be as fast as lightnin' ... Not as good as Roo, when he's fit, mind yer, but he could run rings round the best of us.' (Barney to Olive, p.23)

'He don't hold no grudges...' (Barney to Roo, about Johnnie, p.54)

'... you and Roo have got a lot in common underneath...' (Barney to Johnnie, p.62)

Johnnie is a minor character in terms of stage time, but his role is very important in terms of plot. He was present at one of the key incidents in the narrative: the moment in the cane fields when Roo's weaknesses became apparent. Johnnie resembles the kind of man Roo must once have been: likeable, strong, a natural leader. When Johnnie meets Bubba we can imagine how the young Roo and Olive might have felt about each other when they met.

Johnnie's youth and success serve to highlight how Roo's age has made him vulnerable in a job where physical strength and capability count for everything. Johnnie is flawed (he did, after all, laugh at Roo when Roo collapsed in the cane fields) but guileless; he is willing to apologise and make amends. He also treats Bubba intelligently and kindly, which encourages the audience to empathise with him.

Q How is Johnnie similar to Roo? In what ways do they differ?

THEMES, IDEAS & VALUES

Tradition

Key quotes

'... it's about time some decent woman took this feller in hand. I don't reckon I've ever heard of anyone with more reasons to get married in all my life.' (p.9)

'But this is the lay-off. You can't go looking for work in the lay-off!' (p.35)

The play explores two senses of the word 'tradition'. It interrogates societal notions of 'traditional' or conventional lifestyles; it also examines the idea of ritual and the traditions that people create for themselves.

Convention

Pearl is the character who most represents traditional societal values in *Summer of the Seventeenth Doll.* In particular, she exhibits a tenacious faith in the institution of marriage. She believes that marriage is the way to straighten out any man, even to the point of hoping that she might eventually be able to manipulate Barney into marrying her. Such an act would be not only for her own benefit, but also to enable him to mend the error of his ways, including his fathering of illegitimate children (for whom she even begins knitting jumpers).

Pearl has no doubt that the traditional custom of marriage is the correct way to maintain long-term romantic relationships. She questions, both explicitly and internally, Olive and Roo's relationship and their lifestyle, saying it isn't 'decent' because it doesn't conform to the social conventions of the day. Not only does she feel that there is something less than decent about the relationship, but she sees herself as being in alignment with the majority of her society, arguing that 'nobody would say it was a decent way of living' (p.13).

Pearl's insistence on accepted tradition and practice is also evident in her mundane housekeeping preferences. For example, when Olive brings out the beer bottles in the first scene, Pearl worries that they will make 'rings on the cloth' if they are placed directly onto the table (p.9), whereas Olive isn't the least bit concerned about this.

In contrast to Pearl, Olive feels free to make her own decisions about what is and isn't appropriate. She has no interest in marriage, claiming that what she has is so much more preferable that even 'waiting for Roo to come back is more exciting' than anything a traditional marriage could offer (p.14). She has weighed up her options and decided that a conventional relationship will not fulfil her, and instead she creates her own traditions within her unconventional life.

By presenting both Pearl's and Olive's perspectives on conventions such as marriage – and by demonstrating that neither character lives 'happily ever after' – the play does not put forward a strong argument either for or against the value of social conventions. Instead it supports the idea that conventions can either restrict or offer guidance, depending on the situation and the personalities of those involved.

Key point

Other characters are more equivocal than Pearl or Olive regarding the ideas of tradition and social convention. The men and Bubba all endorse the less conventional lifestyle, but they are less passionately committed to it than Olive.

Ritual

The play is constructed around the notion of ritual. At its heart is the ritual of the dolls: established and perpetuated by Olive and Roo, and eventually destroyed by Roo. Along with this particularly poignant symbolic ritual are many other traditions, such as spending New Year's Eve with Nancy's cousins the Morrises; or visiting Selby at Christmas; or even the 'Sunday night boat trips up the river' (p.49). These rituals are the things Olive clings to, as she watches her familiar lay-off lifestyle slowly slip away from her during this seventeenth summer.

One important idea presented by the play is that rituals can be meaningful and comforting, but they must ultimately change or come to an end. The key value this idea endorses is that of flexibility. Olive, the character most doggedly attached to her unchanging traditions, is also the character who is most damaged by the loss of these rituals.

Q What other traditions does Olive cling to from past lay-offs? Do other characters value these rituals as much as she does?

Expectations and disillusionment

Key quotes

'Oh, I'm not anticipating anythin', believe me.' (Pearl, p.9)

'Honest, she boosted you two up so much before you came, I didn't know what to expect–' (Pearl, p.49)

'There's not one thing I've found here been anything like what you told me.' (Pearl, p.77)

'... there's no more flyin' down out of the sun – no more eagles ... This is the dust we're in and we're gunna walk through it like everyone else for the rest of our lives!' (Roo, p.93)

Summer of the Seventeenth Doll warns against the dangers of building up expectations. Lawler regularly puts his characters in situations where they have high hopes for their immediate or long-term future, and then explores their responses when these hopes are dashed. The result is always a let-down; no characters' expectations are exceeded, or even fulfilled. Instead, we are taught that ambitions that are not grounded in reality inevitably lead to disappointment.

In the most explicit illustration of this theme, Olive has pinned her expectations on 'five months of heaven' (p.13) every year for sixteen years. This year, when everything changes, she is disillusioned almost to the point of collapse. However, the other characters also have to deal with the consequences of their hopes and dreams being unfulfilled.

Even though Pearl claims she isn't anticipating anything, she has internalised Olive's joyful appraisals of past summers, leading her to expect something of the carefree and pleasurable lay-off that Olive has enjoyed for sixteen years. This expectation is firmly squashed; the weather, the reality of the holiday house in Selby and Pearl's own high standards conspire to present a series of unsatisfying (at least to Pearl) summer outings. Her cautious hopes about a relationship with Barney, too, are left unfulfilled.

Of all the characters, Barney seems the least beset by disappointment. He rarely reveals specific hopes and expectations; he regularly changes his priorities in order to fit in with the situation. For example, after initial resistance he considers getting a job in the city. However, towards the end we realise that his disillusionment has already happened: he lost Nancy when she married Harry.

Roo, too, experiences disappointment. His normal way of life has ended, but he tries to make the best of it, proposing to Olive so that they can settle down and enjoy each other's company. He is disillusioned, yet he seeks to remake his life and plan for the future. When Olive refuses him, Roo is left hopeless, alone and directionless.

Bubba hopes for a life like Olive has had, only without the eventual disappointment when things must change. Lawler does not show us Bubba's disillusionment, but the events of the play give us reason to suspect that despite (or perhaps because of) her youthful faith and optimism, she too will experience the disappointments of hopes unfulfilled.

Emma forms a strong contrast with the other characters, since she rarely hopes for anything better than she has. Occasionally, though, even she sometimes hopes for things which never come to fruition. For example, she thinks they might have an enjoyable sing-song, but this quickly falls to pieces because nobody is able to fulfil her expectations of high musical standards and concentration (pp.50–2).

Although the play shows so many expectations which are never fulfilled, it also implies that the characters' hopes have been rewarded in the past. Olive, for example, has good reason to expect a wonderful lay-off season: she has had sixteen before now. The play, then, endorses the value of realism, as opposed to optimism. There is nothing wrong with hopes and dreams, as long as one is prepared to accept reality, which so often falls short of expectations. The underlying idea is that blind optimism inevitably leads to disappointment.

Key point

Although *Summer of the Seventeenth Doll* suggests that expectations always lead to disappointment, this does not mean that it argues that life is hopeless. Instead, it endorses pragmatism: a position of recognising the likelihood that reality will differ from hopes and dreams. The play also suggests that it is our own expectations and responses, rather than the events themselves, which determine how distressed or overwhelmed we become at such disillusionment.

Q Can you find an example in the play of a character exhibiting realistic expectations?

Q Do you agree that building up expectations will ultimately lead to disappointment, or do you think that the play presents an overly negative view of the world?

Coming of age and impermanence

Key quotes

'Nancy got out while the going was good...' (Emma, p.81)

'Nobody tells me I'm old. I'm as good a man now as ever I was.' (Roo, p.82)

'How long did you think these lay-off seasons were gunna last – forever? They're not for keeps, you know; these are just – seasons.' (Emma, p.82)

'Little Bubba – you've outgrown the lot of us, haven't you?' (Roo, pp.86–7)

It is significant that the summer portrayed is that of the seventeenth doll, as the eighteenth year of life is often seen as the final year of childhood. In Australia, as in many other countries, eighteen is the age of majority, or the age at which an individual is legally responsible for themselves. Although the central characters are adults, collectively their narrative is on the precipice of adulthood and the pattern of lay-off seasons is about to come of age. This final summer of youth, carrying connotations of innocence, freedom and optimism, ushers in the changes normally implied by adulthood: responsibility, obligations, the relinquishment of a certain degree of idealism, and an expectation of 'settling' at some point.

As Katharine Brisbane observes in her essay 'Growing up in Australia', contained in the 1978 Currency Press edition of the play, *The Doll* is not just an illustration of the coming of age of individual characters, but, broader still, of a nation. Brisbane argues that 'The 1950s was a crucial period in the development of the Australian identity' and that the play on one level reflects this national period of 'growing up' (p.ix).

Literal age

Bubba and, to a lesser extent, Johnnie are the two characters who represent the literal transition from youth into adulthood. Bubba, thanks to her history with the Leeches and the canecutters, has to fight hard to gain recognition as an adult from them. Barney inadvertently offers her an extra resource in her struggle when he introduces her to Johnnie. Roo and others joke about Bubba's age, but by the end of the play she shows that she is capable of making her own choices. There is a certain sadness implicated in her letting go of her childlike identity: after Johnnie's lead, presumably she will come to be known as

Kathie rather than Bubba, and with 'Bubba' will go the childish joys of dolls, candy walking-sticks and the freedom to run in and out of the Leeches' house. Kathie's concerns will be more 'adult' and serious. For example, she will have to find a way to maintain the kind of joyful life she has previously witnessed between Olive and Roo, without letting 'breaking things and ... arguments' (p.86) get in the way.

Symbolic age

For the characters in *The Doll,* the lay-off seasons are about to come of age, but judging by the events of the play, the eighteenth summer – the first summer of adulthood – will not be one of celebration, as literal eighteenth birthdays tend to be. Instead, it will mark the first year in a new reality for all the characters. The carefree days of their 'youth' (the first sixteen summers) have undeniably ended, as Emma asserts: 'The layoffs in this house are finished – for all of you' (p.94). And with what will they be replaced? The play does not seek to answer this question. The characters do not know what they face in the future, only that it will be different from the familiar routines of their past. This is much like the experience of entering adulthood: we never know exactly what to expect, but we know with certainty that there will be changes ahead, and that we cannot go backwards.

Key point

The idea implicit in the play's symbolic representation of the transition into adulthood is that nothing stays the same forever. Different characters come to terms with this in different ways; some, like Olive, are unable to deal with it. Others, like Barney, make new plans and move on to other stages of life.

This theme introduces the value of growth: life is about accepting change and adapting to new circumstances. The play suggests that dealing positively with such changes – growing and learning from experience, rather than being crippled by it – enables us to make the most of life.

The only character who seems to have completely escaped the devastating effects of change is Nancy. Although we never meet Nancy, the characters' many references to her indicate that she was able to enjoy the youthful summers past, and to move into a new phase of life before everything fell down around her. This supports the view that adapting to change can mitigate its damaging effects. Nancy seems to have exhibited a maturity that few other characters possess, in her ability to anticipate and manage change.

Q How does the play argue that we must prepare ourselves for change?

Q The play seems to mourn the loss of youth. Does it also suggest that leaving behind youthful dreams is a necessary and fulfilling part of life? Justify your answer.

Friendship

Key quotes

'You know what Roo's always been to me, a sort of little tin god.' (Barney to Olive, p.24)

'ROO: I don't want your money, I can still earn my own. *[Bitingly]* Even if I have got a busted back.

BARNEY: *[stung]* You pig-headed mug. What about all those times you've carried me – every year when I've run dry down here you've kicked me on...' (p.35)

'I reckon the only way out for both of us is to split up for a while.' (Barney to Roo, p.88)

Summer of the Seventeenth Doll is the story of the sad ending of an era for Olive and her lifestyle, but it is also the ending of an era for Roo and Barney, who have enjoyed a twenty-year friendship. We first hear of the men as inseparable mates who have been successful canecutters and welcome visitors in the Leech household for sixteen summers, but throughout the play we see the strains that the years have placed on their friendship. Through the financial and emotional trials of this seventeenth year, the play charts the decline of their friendship, even though both make efforts (particularly towards the end) to overcome their antagonism and rebuild their relationship. In the very final moments as they make eye contact before exiting the stage, *'there is no bravado or questing hope, it is a completely open acknowledgement of what they have lost'* (p.95). When they leave the house a moment later, it is clear that it is for the last time and that this part of their lives is over.

The play also explores other friendships, such as that between Olive and Bubba (similar to an aunt/niece relationship), and between Olive and Pearl (a somewhat terse, fragile relationship). While Roo and Barney's is the most dramatic and significant, all the friendships in *Summer of the Seventeenth Doll* experience dramatic change, mostly for the worse. Even the friendship with Nancy, which we only hear of through characters' reminiscences, has ended. Her decision to leave the group has completely alienated her, and there are no hints that there will be any reunion in the future between Nancy and any of the other characters.

Without being overtly negative or pessimistic, the play seems to suggest that friendship cannot be relied upon as a permanent source of emotional security. The play's events indicate that friendship is unlikely to be enduring, but that an individual's capacity to grow and adapt can help them to accept change. Olive clings to her friendships, unable to acknowledge their transformation and decline over time, and as a result is greatly distressed by their impermanence. Conversely, Nancy, as far as we know, did not experience great trauma at leaving the group. Rather, she judged that the time had come to make a change, because she no longer shared the necessary values and qualities with the others to maintain her relationship with them.

An underlying idea is that friendship is often based on similarity (whether of circumstances or of values and desires). As a result, when people's circumstances change, or their values begin to diverge (as in the case of Roo and Barney), friendships can suffer.

Q Why do the characters in *The Doll* fail to maintain successful friendships? Are such failures unique to the heightened stress of this situation, or do you think Lawler is suggesting that friendship is ephemeral?

Q Why do you think Olive could not continue her friendship with Nancy after her departure and marriage?

Loyalty

Key quotes

'They don't have to write me, I know where they are.' (Olive to Pearl, p.14)

'But that was the only time I ever slipped. I've stood by you other times, haven't I?' (Barney to Roo, p.55)

'... what d'yer reckon Olive does in that time? Knocks around with other blokes, goes out on the loose every week? No, she doesn't, she just waits for us to come back again ... I couldn't let her down...' (Roo to Barney, pp.55–6)

The ideas of friendship and loyalty are interconnected but also distinct. In *The Doll* the value of loyalty is endorsed, even though loyalty is not enough to prevent the demise of friendships, relationships and lifestyles. One way for a text to endorse a particular value is to demonstrate that the characters who uphold this value are rewarded, either through the fulfilment of their desires or through positive outcomes for these characters. However, *Summer of the Seventeenth Doll* does not offer happy endings for any of its characters. If the play does not show that loyalty is capable of protecting friendships and relationships, how does Lawler argue that loyalty is important?

There are several instances in the play where characters discuss the value of loyalty, either explicitly or implicitly. These include:

- Olive's explanation to Pearl of the arrangement with Roo in the times between the lay-offs (p.14), which conveys her belief that she can trust him completely
- Olive's disappointment when Roo reveals his plans to stay with a cousin since he is broke, even though Olive does not judge his financial situation and assumes that he will still come to her as he has always done (pp.25–6)
- Emma's acknowledgement that even though Roo hasn't married her daughter, he has been constant to her for seventeen years (p.34)
- Barney and Pearl's discussion about Barney's illegitimate children (pp.38–40)
- Roo and Barney's discussion about Roo walking off on the gang (p.55)

- Roo's outburst to Barney about how Olive waits for him between lay-offs (pp.55–6)
- the ongoing implication that by leaving to get married, Nancy somehow let down the others in the group.

In each of these instances, we see that the characters value and respect loyalty in themselves and others. Olive and Roo firmly defend their relationship and each other's loyalty (which Emma also acknowledges), each asserting that the other is trustworthy and respecting the fact that they wait for each other throughout the cutting season until they can be together again.

Barney argues his own case in front of the judging Pearl, proud of the reliable and enduring support that he has offered to his children. When it comes to his friendship with Roo, Barney prides himself on only having let Roo down on one occasion; unfortunately, this was the one time when Roo felt that Barney's loyalty was really required. So although loyalty cannot offer Olive and Roo's relationship or Roo and Barney's friendship immunity against disintegration, the play still subtly argues that loyalty is a desirable trait; without it, neither the relationship nor the friendship could have survived as long as they did.

These examples also demonstrate how people are hurt when others lack loyalty.

Feelings of pain and loss are evident, too, in the characters' responses to Nancy's absence from the group. Though none of the characters criticise her, they have all been hurt by her departure and by her and Barney's inability to sustain their relationship. There is no blame laid upon either character, but there is a sadness in the group, as Bubba articulates: 'It's awful to think of the two of them, feeling like they do, and yet messing it up' (p.32). In the very first conversation of the play, Bubba says, though without resentment, that she thinks Nancy 'got tired of waiting' (p.5). She didn't have the loyal patience that Olive has. When she left, Olive and the men couldn't bring themselves to go to her wedding, or to visit her cousins for New Year's Eve; they can barely even discuss her. Although it is never explicitly stated, there is the implied suggestion that had Nancy been able to 'wait' loyally, she and Barney might still be together.

This theme is an interesting example of the subtle, implicit ways that a text can endorse particular societal values and views. The idea of loyalty underlies many of the relationships and, ultimately, the conflicts in the play, yet it is rarely discussed openly, and it does not result in 'happily ever after' endings even for those characters whose loyalty is most constant.

Q What other social values are endorsed implicitly in the play?

Q Does Lawler provide any textual evidence to argue *against* the value of loyalty?

Masculinity

Key quotes

'... you can't compare them ... Roo's the big man of the two, but it's Barney makes you laugh.' (Olive to Pearl, p.11)

'These are men, not the sort we see go rolling home to their wives every night, but men ... they'd walk into the pub as if they owned it ... the regulars'd stand aside to let 'em through, just as if they was a – a coupla kings.' (Olive to Pearl, pp.14–15)

'D'yer want him to think I'm scared?' (Roo to Olive, p.59)

The men in the play embody a certain form of an idealised Australian male. Both Roo and Barney are:

- physically strong and competent (even though age is beginning to compromise Roo's superiority)
- mentally resilient, or trying hard to be
- employed as physical labourers

- successful with women (particularly Barney)
- well-liked and respected socially
- tough and yet also compassionate at times
- disinclined to talk about emotions
- determined not to give in to vulnerabilities.

The play examines threats to some of these elements of masculinity, and explores the men's struggles to respond effectively to those threats. For Roo, the main threat is the diminishing of his physical strength and the loss of his position of leadership within the canecutting society. He is forced to show his new weakness and vulnerability in front of Johnnie, effectively a competitor for Roo's role; his sense that this is virtually an admission of utter failure only compounds his feelings of powerlessness.

The main threat to Barney's masculinity is his waning power over women. It is not just Pearl whom he fails to woo but, as Roo points out in an argument, 'two waitresses at the Greek café' as well as a number of other anonymous women and, most hurtfully, Nancy herself (p.74). Just as Roo's masculinity is bound up in his physical superiority, Barney's masculinity is entangled with his natural ability to win over any woman whom he chooses. He keeps up a pretence that he is as competent and irresistible as ever, but Roo's accusations suggest otherwise. We see that with age, both men's measures of themselves are now falling short of their own standards of masculinity.

The play implies that masculinity is an important value in society, and that, rightly or wrongly, there are certain criteria by which we judge masculinity. One idea embodied in the text is that men should fight against emasculation. The play also explores the difficulties such narrow expectations of men can cause, both for individuals and for the wider society.

Q The Australian male ideal that Roo, particularly, represents is not confined to the 1950s. Some contemporary beer advertisements on television, for example, endorse similar values of masculinity: physical prowess, outdoor occupations, loyalty combined with a sense of wildness. How relevant do you think this image is today?

Q How does the play show us the importance of this idealised form of masculinity in the society of the time? Does it also show its flaws and limitations?

DIFFERENT INTERPRETATIONS

Different interpretations arise from different responses to a text. These responses can be published in newspapers, journals and books, both online and in print, by critics and reviewers. They can also be expressed in discussions among readers in the media, classrooms, book groups and so on. A production of a play is also an interpretation of the text (the script), and reviews respond to the original script as well as to the production. While there is no single correct reading or interpretation of a text, it is important to understand that an interpretation is more than an 'opinion' – it is the justification of a point of view on the text. To present an interpretation of the text based on your point of view you must use a logical argument and support it with relevant evidence from the text.

Contemporary reception

In a 2011 article discussing the longevity of *Summer of the Seventeenth Doll,* Steve Meacham notes that the play is considered a 'pivotal moment in Australian theatre': one of the first truly Australian works to be produced on the Australian stage, which was in the 1950s accustomed to presenting works from elsewhere. Though its first production toured in London and the United States, it didn't receive quite the same success overseas (especially in the US) as it did at home, where it spoke to an audience who understood the world Lawler was presenting. *The Doll* has continued to receive critical acclaim for its contemporary Australian productions, and as an important literary and dramatic work. Contemporary critics of productions tend to argue that the play continues to have validity; as reviewer Cameron Woodhead says of the 2012 Melbourne Theatre Company production, the play remains 'as potent' and 'as relevant today as when it was written'.

Theatre critic Alison Croggon (in an extended response inspired by the same MTC production) goes so far as to call it 'the most famous Australian play ever written or produced'. She discusses its strength and importance, even though, interestingly, she herself doesn't necessarily think it is 'a great play'. (This is a good example of how a personal *opinion* does not prevent an informed and balanced *analysis.)* She argues that even though any number of other Australian works might be more important theatrically and as literature, *The Doll* retains its 'classic' status and its right to be considered a pivotal Australian work by virtue of its durability and capacity to communicate with contemporary audiences.

Two possible interpretations

This section contains two contrasting interpretations of *Summer of the Seventeenth Doll.* They provide examples of how evidence from the text can be used to support differing and even conflicting interpretations of the play. This reminds us that characters, events and other textual evidence do not necessarily present black-and-white viewpoints or ideas. Just as we all respond differently to a text, we can find different ways of responding to the same textual element, such as the development of a character or a specific incident.

Reading 1

The character of Bubba shows us that we are not all destined for disappointment and loss, and that there is hope for the future.

While the majority of the characters in *Summer of the Seventeenth Doll* are portrayed as being past their prime and entering into a phase of their lives which is characterised by disappointment and loss, the two younger characters, Bubba and Johnnie, offer a different perspective on life. Bubba, particularly, is carefully constructed so that even though she is a minor character in terms of stage time, she is able to balance the sad pessimism embodied by the other characters. Bubba shows that there are other possibilities in life and that the end of the lay-off lifestyle for Olive, Roo, Barney and Nancy is not necessarily the inescapable pattern of life for everyone.

The fate of the three central characters (and the absent Nancy) seems inevitable – there are no points in the play at which we see how they might have prevented the dissolution of their carefree lay-off/canecutting season way of life. There is no suggestion that things could have been done differently; the ultimate disappointment for each of these characters results from their efforts to cling to the life they believe in (though this differs slightly for Roo, who attempts to make changes yet wants to remain with Olive). Without Bubba in the picture, the play would present an unremittingly cynical perspective on the world: nothing good ever lasts, and we all end up alone, no matter what we do. Even Emma has ended up alone, though we never hear how or why.

Bubba, however, is a source of optimism among all this hopelessness. In her youthfulness she offers an energetic, positive view of the world. Her first line informs us that she was the only one of the friends to go to Nancy's wedding – while the others could not bring themselves to go, she was able to embrace and celebrate Nancy's happiness, even when it meant her departure from the group.

Bubba regularly demonstrates that while she respects and enjoys the traditions that the group of friends has established, she is not bound by them (in the inflexible way that Olive is, for example). Instead, she is willing to embrace changes and alternatives. Consider the irritable confinement of the four older characters, playing cards and knitting on New Year's Eve. They will not go to the Morrises' because they can't accept that Nancy has left the group, and the Morrises' would be a reminder of past years. Bubba easily finds somewhere else to go, happy to celebrate the night and prepared to welcome new experiences. Similarly, while she is happy to perpetuate childish traditions such as the lolly walking-sticks she gives to Roo and Barney every year, she is also keen to grow up and to move on to new stages of life. This willingness to move on is exemplified by her delight at Johnnie's use of her real name (Kathie) instead of her old affectionate nickname which is starting to trap her in a youth she no longer wishes to embody. Bubba recognises that change is inevitable, and embraces this idea, which suggests that she will not suffer the same disappointments as other characters. Compare Bubba's attitude to that of Olive, who hopelessly clings to the symbolically childish kewpie doll tradition and, when it is destroyed, bitterly mourns the loss.

When Bubba welcomes Johnnie (in many ways a younger version of Roo) into her world, she seems in danger of following in Olive's footsteps and living a similar life, which would surely lead to similar despair in the future. However, Bubba is firm in her energetic belief that she can avoid such an end: she tells Roo that she will work hard to have the same joyous lay-off lifestyle with its independence and its certainties of seasonal returns, but 'have it differently ... have it safe and know that it's going to last' (p.86). Her optimism in the final moments of the play conveys hope that each of us can control our own fate and, with flexibility and openness, avoid the emotional devastation and loss suffered in the end by Roo, Barney, Pearl and Olive.

Reading 2

The character of Bubba enhances the tragedy of *Summer of the Seventeenth Doll* : although she is young and idealistic, the events of the play show us that

her path through life is unlikely to differ from Olive's.

Summer of the Seventeenth Doll portrays a tragic turning point in the lives of a group of friends: they have enjoyed a blissful existence for sixteen years, but in this seventeenth summer all their hopes come crashing down, leaving each of them broken and alone. Bubba, who can be seen as a younger version of Olive, serves to make this tragedy all the more powerful. In her youth and optimism, she believes that she will be able to enjoy the same blissful existence, yet avoid the downfall. But in a cruel dramatic irony, the audience can see what Bubba cannot: her similarity to Olive, and her desire to enjoy the same lay-off lifestyle, suggests that she cannot help but follow the same path and that she will find herself, many years later, in just the same situation as Olive.

At first, we see Bubba as a symbol of hope. We are convinced by her cheery optimism, and charmed by her affection for the cutters and for the way of life that the friends have led. As the play progresses and we see that Olive is trapped in a disintegrating fantasy of her own making, there is hope that Bubba will be able to avoid this fate. She is emerging into society as a bright young woman, and Johnnie Dowd's affection for her is full of promise. He sees her for who she really is, not simply as the kid-next-door that Olive and the men have fondly known for so long. His refusal to use her nickname, insisting instead on calling her Kathie, is empowering, leading the audience to feel hope for their blossoming relationship.

Gradually, however, we realise that Bubba and Johnnie's relationship is likely to be very similar to Olive and Roo's. Johnnie, like Roo, is a virile young canecutter who, we can assume, will follow in Roo's footsteps, living half the year up north and spending the lay-offs with Bubba. Bubba, for her part, has been so bewitched by Olive and Roo's relationship and the pattern of the lay-off seasons that she hopes her own life will be just the same. Roo recognises this, saying that they have 'spoilt' for her any ambitions of living life in another way, and she agrees, saying 'nothin' else is any good, that's all' (p.86). This gives us no reason to hope that she will settle, like Nancy, and step out of the cycle of lay-offs before it damages her in the way it damages Olive.

Bubba's own impending situation is all the more painful because we can see how it could be otherwise: she has the time and opportunity to shape her life in a way that would avoid a sad end like Olive's, but she has no desire to. While we mourn Olive and Roo's loss, it seems an inevitable consequence of a chain of events set in motion long ago. We see Bubba at her most youthful and optimistic, but we know that these qualities will not last. This heightens the tragedy of *The Doll,* suggesting that no matter how optimistically we begin, we can never end as we might hope.

QUESTIONS & ANSWERS

This section focuses on your own analytical writing on the text, and gives you strategies for producing high quality responses in your coursework and exam essays.

Essay writing – an overview

An essay on a literary work is a formal and serious piece of writing that presents your point of view on the text, usually in response to a given topic. Your 'point of view' in an essay is your interpretation of the meaning of the text's language, structure, characters, situations and events, supported by detailed analysis of textual evidence.

Analyse – don't summarise

In your essays it is important to avoid simply summarising what happens in a text:

- A **summary** is a description or paraphrase (retelling in different words) of the characters and events. For example: 'Macbeth has a horrifying vision of a dagger dripping with blood before he goes to murder King Duncan'.
- An **analysis** is an explanation of the real meaning or significance that lies 'beneath' the text's words (and images, for a film).

For example: 'Macbeth's vision of a bloody dagger shows how deeply uneasy he is about the violent act he is contemplating – as well as his sense that supernatural forces are impelling him to act'.

A limited amount of summary is sometimes necessary to let your reader know which part of the text you wish to discuss. However, always keep this to a minimum and follow it immediately with your analysis (explanation) of what this part of the text is really telling us.

Plan your essay

Carefully plan your essay so that you have a clear idea of what you are going to say. The plan ensures that your ideas flow logically, that your argument remains consistent and that you stay on the topic. An essay plan should be a list of **brief dot points** – no more than half a page.

- Include your central argument or main contention – a concise statement (usually in a single sentence) of your overall response to the topic. See 'Analysing a sample topic' for guidelines on how to formulate a main contention.
- Write three or four dot points for each paragraph indicating the main idea and evidence/examples from the text. Note that in

your essay you will need to *expand* on these points and *analyse* the evidence.

Structure your essay

An essay is a complete, self-contained piece of writing. It has a clear beginning (the introduction), middle (several body paragraphs) and end (the last paragraph or conclusion). It must also have a central argument that runs throughout, linking each paragraph to form a coherent whole.

See examples of introductions and conclusions in the 'Analysing a sample topic' and 'Sample answer' sections.

The introduction establishes your overall response to the topic. It includes your main contention and outlines the main evidence you will refer to in the course of the essay. Write your introduction *after* you have done a plan and *before* you write the rest of the essay.

The body paragraphs argue your case – they present evidence from the text and explain how this evidence supports your argument. Each body paragraph needs:

- a strong **topic sentence** (usually the first sentence) that states the main point being made in the paragraph
- **evidence** from the text, including some brief quotations

- **analysis** of the textual evidence explaining its significance and **explanation** of how it supports your argument
- **links back to the topic** in one or more statements, usually towards the end of the paragraph.

Connect the body paragraphs so that your discussion flows smoothly. Use some linking words and phrases like 'similarly' and 'on the other hand', though don't start every paragraph like this. Another strategy is to use a significant word from the last sentence of one paragraph in the first sentence of the next.

Use key terms from the topic – or similes for them – throughout, so the relevance of your discussion to the topic is always clear.

The conclusion ties everything together and finishes the essay. It includes strong statements that emphasise your central argument and provide a clear response to the topic.

Avoid simply restating the points made earlier in the essay – this will end on a very flat note and imply that you have run out of ideas and vocabulary. The conclusion is meant to be a logical extension of what you have written, not just a repetition or summary. Writing an effective conclusion can be a challenge. Try using these tips:

- Start by linking back to the final sentence of the second-last paragraph – this helps your writing to 'flow', rather than just leaping back to your main contention straight away.

- Use similes and expressions with equivalent meanings to vary your vocabulary. This allows you to reinforce your line of argument without being repetitive.
- When planning your essay, think of one or two broad statements or observations about the text's wider meaning. These should be related to the topic and your overall argument. Keep them for the conclusion, since they will give you something 'new' to say but still follow logically from your discussion. The introduction will be focused on the topic, but the conclusion can present a wider view of the text.

Essay topics

1 When Olive tries to dust the dolls, birds and butterflies, they disintegrate so that she cannot replace them. How does Lawler use symbolism to illuminate his themes?

2 '*Summer of the Seventeenth Doll* is a celebration of youth.' Discuss.

3 Emma calls Roo and Barney "two of a pair" (p.83). How alike are Roo and Barney?

4 '*Summer of the Seventeenth Doll* is a play about the inevitability of disappointment.' Discuss.

5 Barney tells Pearl that a woman needs three things to be able to live with a man like himself, but he never tells her the third, saying merely that he's "only ever met one woman who had [it] ... And even she didn't have enough to keep the two of us together" (p.79). What do you think it is that Nancy had and Pearl does not?

6 'Bubba and Johnnie are a younger version of Olive and Roo, and their relationship will inevitably end in the same way.' Discuss.

7 'Pearl is brought in as a replacement for Nancy, but instead she inadvertently acts as the catalyst for the ending of the lay-offs.' Discuss.

8 Alison Croggon calls *The Doll* 'a startlingly well-written text, of its time and place, but resonating beyond them'. How well do the play's themes speak to a contemporary audience?

9 Emma says, "... that's all very fine and a lot of fun while it lasts, but last is one thing it just don't do" (p.83). Are you convinced by Emma's argument, and the events of the play, that good things cannot last?

10 'Olive is the most important character in the play.' Discuss.

Vocabulary for writing on Summer of the Seventeenth Doll

Dramatic irony: A tension created by the fact that the audience is able to observe and foresee things the characters do not have knowledge of. For example, we know from the start – most simply from the play's title – that this summer will not be like those in the past, but Olive and Bubba do not expect anything to be different.

Exposition: A theatrical term describing the presentation of background information about characters and past events, especially during the opening scenes of a play.

Initiating action or ***inciting incident:*** An event which disturbs the equilibrium of the characters and/or their relationships, generating the further conflict and action of the play.

Naturalism: Originally a theatrical movement in the late nineteenth to early twentieth century, with quite specific guide-lines regarding content and style. Naturalism has come to be used as a general term to describe a realistic style of writing/perfor-mance.

Rising action and ***falling action:*** Descriptions for the narrative development occurring on either side of the climax. (The rising action precedes the climax; the falling action follows it.)

Symbolism: The use of symbols (objects, images, incidents, etc.) to represent other ideas and meanings. For example, in *Summer of the Seventeenth Doll,* when Olive hears a story about migratory birds, she latches onto the idea of eagles flying south for the mating season. The eagles in Olive's analogy symbolise Roo and Barney, who also travel south each year; by choosing eagles rather than any other birds, Olive attributes qualities of nobility and strength to Roo and Barney.

Vernacular: The language, speech and expressions of a particular time and place, or section of society. Can be used as a noun or an adjective: for example, 'the Australian vernacular is central in *The Doll'* or 'Barney's vernacular conversational style informs us about his character.'

Analysing a sample topic

When Olive tries to dust the dolls, birds and butterflies, they disintegrate so that she cannot replace them. How does Lawler use symbolism to illuminate his themes?

A good first step in analysing a topic is to identify and underline the most important terms. This is a complex essay topic with two distinct elements: it identifies a key moment in the play, and then invites you to relate this moment to a broader analysis of the work.

The most important terms occur in the second element: 'symbolism', 'illustrate' and 'themes'. These terms don't function in isolation, so you will need to refer back to the first half of the topic in order to make sense of them. In this case, the first statement describes a particular concrete incident in the play; the second invites you to consider the symbolic meaning of that incident. With your knowledge of the play and its themes, you will recognise that 'dolls', 'disintegrate' and 'cannot replace' are important recurring motifs in the text, and therefore important terms in this topic.

Next you will need to make sure you understand what the topic is asking you to do. It can be useful to simplify and rephrase the requirements in your own words. For example, you might say something like 'provide examples of symbolism, such as Olive losing the decorations, and explain how they help us understand themes such as loss'.

Once you are clear about the topic's demands, you can decide on your overall response and form a main contention. For some topics you will need to decide whether or not you agree with the statement (or, more challengingly, you may wish to argue both sides). In the topic above, however, you are not invited to *disagree* that Lawler uses symbolism; rather, you need to gather evidence from the text that will support your argument about *how* Lawler uses symbolism.

A good way to begin would be to go through the play and list each instance of symbolism, then note a theme that each instance helps to illustrate or develop. Narrow the list down to the strongest examples (those allowing the most in-depth analysis), and plan or outline your response. An example of a paragraph outline is below.

Sample introduction

Although *Summer of the Seventeenth Doll* is a realist drama which presents its characters, situations and events naturalistically, Lawler also harnesses the literary technique of symbolism: a heightened use of narrative imagery which lends the play richness and allows it to work on multiple levels. For example, although Olive takes down physical objects in the final act, the birds, butterflies and – especially – the dolls also stand for her relationship with Roo and the lay-off seasons as a whole.

When they fall apart we see a visual and emotional representation of an important theme already familiar to us from the action and dialogue: the inevitability of good things coming to an end. Olive can no more repair her relationship with Roo, or preserve the lay-off lifestyle, than she can replace the broken ornaments and souvenirs. The symbolism here powerfully communicates the play's central themes.

Body paragraph outline

Paragraph 1 – introduce further examples of symbolism in the play, such as:

- The use of lighting to establish mood and feeling. Refer to specific stage directions, e.g. *'a glowing interior luminosity protected from the drabness outside'* (p.4) This way of lighting the stage can be seen as symbolic of the cheerful optimism that the house and its residents offer at the start of the summer. Note that the stage direction for the final scene does not mention lighting at all, although every other scene has a stage direction for lighting.
- The image of Roo and Barney as eagles flying out of the sun for the mating season (p.48). This symbolises not just the men's itinerant lifestyle, but their virility, strength and freedom.

- The physical conflict between Roo and Barney at the end of Act Two, Scene Two. This is a symbol for the intense emotional and psychological conflict that now exists between them.

Paragraph 2 – explain how the examples in the previous paragraph are able to shed light on various themes.

- The lighting often suggests the emotional tone of a scene. In the example above, the play begins with optimism and ends with an empty hopelessness. One theme supported by the lighting is the disillusionment that accompanies a coming of age.
- The symbolism of the eagles illustrates the theme that change is inevitable and physical prowess is transient. Although Olive clings to her fantasy of the young cutters' strength, Pearl's scorn for the story reminds us that the men are now ageing and failing, and that the glory of their youth is a thing of the past.
- The very explicit symbol of the fight helps us understand the underlying theme of friendship in the play; it is only because of the men's long friendship that their feelings of betrayal and loss are so intense.

Paragraph 3 – discuss how symbolism enables themes to be presented more powerfully and with greater complexity.

- Symbolic representations allow for reiteration of a theme through multiple levels of information: the ideas are communicated not just through concrete use of language in the characters' dialogue, but also through visual and emotional languages. For example, the physical presence of the dolls or the emotional states created by the lighting help us understand the wider meanings of the characters' speech and actions.
- Symbolism in the theatre allows even naturalistic plays to incorporate theatrical elements, capitalising on the capacity of the medium and the form to communicate in ways beyond the linguistic.

Sample conclusion

The use of symbolism allows Lawler to present his themes in more compelling and engaging ways. In fact, the title and the overall setting of the play offer symbolic representations of many of its central themes. The dolls represent the youthful, playful optimism with which the characters begin the play, as well as the theme of growing up. The repetition of the sixteen summers hints at the themes of tradition and ritual; the summer season is symbolic of both the freedoms of the past lay-offs, and also the *heat* or intensity that this lay-off will bring. Through the use of symbolism in powerful moments, such as when Olive is faced with the disintegration of her beloved decorations, Lawler deepens the meaning and impact of his play.

SAMPLE ANSWER

***'Summer of the Seventeenth Doll* is a celebration of youth.' Discuss.**

While *Summer of the Seventeenth Doll* portrays some of the pleasures of carefree youth, this is only as a backdrop to the disappointments, disillusionment and ultimate devastation that accompanies growing up and coming of age. The seventeenth summer of the title suggests the final summer before adulthood; far from being a time of celebration, though, this final summer is overshadowed by the adulthood to come. We see Roo, Barney and especially Olive coming to terms with the loss of the happy-go-lucky lay-off seasons they've enjoyed in the past, and with the ending of relationships that have lasted for sixteen years. While at face value the play might appear to be a celebration of youth, it is rather a meditation on the inevitable demise of youth.

The Doll sets up a strong dichotomy between youth and age, with youth always portrayed as the preferable state. This is evident at a general level, for example in the descriptions Olive has offered Pearl of the past summers as an idyllic panorama of river trips, parties and fun. The other extreme of life, as represented by the elderly Emma, is characterised by irritability, miserliness and only occasional entertainment such as the community singing. The youth/age division is also illustrated by Bubba and Olive. At twenty-two, Bubba has the freedom and opportunity to steer her life in a direction of her own choosing, and the optimism to believe that she will continue to wield this power. Olive, on the other hand, increasingly recognises that she is losing control over the turns her life will take. She cannot help Roo financially, and she ultimately cannot hold on to the rituals and patterns of life that she loves so deeply. Age, for Olive, brings only disillusionment.

The canecutters, too, clearly illustrate the differences between youth and age, this time through a contrast of their younger selves with their present selves. Both Roo and Barney have been successful, respected and attractive men: Roo a superb physical labourer, and Barney a larrikin with great appeal to women. Throughout the play, though, we see how their age has reduced their respective talents. In the previous season Roo struggled in the cane fields, unable to dominate as in the past and eventually humiliated in front of his gang. Barney, in turn, is unable to secure Pearl as a partner, and has recently been rejected by a number of women in various bars and shops. In Roo's case there is an extra illustration of the cruelty of age: while his physical prowess diminishes, we are introduced to young Johnnie Dowd, whose youth allows him to easily surpass Roo in the cane fields. The men's physical decline impacts not only on their individual senses of masculinity and self-worth, but also on their twenty-year friendship, causing a loss of trust and a deep questioning of loyalty, which in turn leads to a spiteful argument and fight. Finally Roo and Barney are forced to leave the house and the lay-off lifestyle, walking away from both the Leech household and, symbolically, the pleasures and optimism of youth. The script clearly suggests that youth is the best part of a life.

However, the emphasis in *The Doll* is never on celebration. The wonderful, carefree days of youth are alluded to merely in order to throw into sharp relief the sorrowful state in which the characters find themselves at the end of this final summer. Instead of arguing that youth should be celebrated, the play conveys the idea that all good things will come to an end, that loss and disappointment are inevitable elements of growing older. In his discussion with Emma in the final scene, for example, Roo wonders whose fault it was that the lay-off season has all gone wrong this year – it is as though he thinks that a few simple mistakes have caused a one-off unhappy summer. Emma, however, asserts that 'All that's happened is you've gone as far as you can go' (p.82). She makes a compelling argument that with age comes an unavoidable loss of freedom, happiness and possibility.

While 'celebrating youth' and 'mourning the loss of youth' appear to simply represent two sides of a single coin, they are quite different in tone. A celebration suggests a positive, optimistic analysis of possibility and potential. Mourning, on the other hand, implies loss and regret; looking back rather than looking forwards; certainties rather than possibilities. *The Doll* works on certainties – change will always occur; happiness can never last – rather than inviting the possibilities of hope and dreams. Thus the play is not a celebration of youth, but a meditation on the ending of youth and the inevitable losses that accompany ageing.

REFERENCES & READING

Text

Lawler, Ray 1978, *Summer of the Seventeenth Doll,* Currency Press, Sydney. First published 1957.

Article, reviews, interviews

Croggon, Alison 2012, 'Olive as Tragic Hero: Summer of the Seventeenth Doll', 1 May, theatrenotes.blogspot.com.au/2012/05/olive-as-tragic-hero-summer-of.html

Meacham, Steve 2011, 'A lucky play', *Sydney Morning Herald,* 3 September, www.smh.com.au/entertainment/theatre/a-lucky-play-20110901-1jmlp.html

Smith, Amanda 2012, 'Interview with Ray Lawler and John Sumner', Radio National, 22 January, www.abc.net.au/radionational/programs/artworks/ray-lawler-and-the-doll/3660980

Woodhead, Cameron 2012, 'Summer of the Seventeenth Doll', *The Age,* 18 January, www.theage.com.au/entertainment/about

-town/summer-of-the-seventeenth-doll-20120117-1q4kq.html

Other references

Cuddon, JA 1988, *Dictionary of Literary Terms and Literary Theory,* Penguin, London.

Lawler, Ray 1978, *The Doll Trilogy,* Currency Press, NSW.

Love, Harold (ed.) 1984, *The Australian Stage: A Documentary History,* NSW University Press, Sydney.

Radic, Leonard 2006, *Contemporary Australian Drama,* Brandl & Schlesinger, Blackheath.

www.ingramcontent.com/pod-product-compliance
Lightning Source LLC
Chambersburg PA
CBHW080301030726
47593CB00009B/2588

* 9 7 8 1 4 5 9 6 6 2 2 4 7 *